Lean Communication

Lean Communication:

Talk Less, Say More

Jack Malcolm

WISDOM/WORKS
Published by Wisdom Works

Ẇ

Published 2021

Copyright © 2021, Jack Malcolm
ISBN 978-1-7365759-2-5

Printed in the United States of America

Set in Adobe Garamond Pro
Designed by Abigail Chiaramonte
Cover Concept by Sara Morris

For
June Frances Simari
and
Henry Willard Malcolm
May you always strive to be of value

Contents

Foreword

Tom Morris

The tremendously insightful ancient philosopher Aristotle understood that the finest things we can accomplish tend to grow out of a certain kind of fertile soil, and arise in a particular way. I think the formula can be described very simply as:

People in Partnership for a Shared Purpose.

Rarely do great things come from a single person operating in isolation from others. The most common source for the good we do involves a multiplicity of people in a particular relationship of creative collaboration, brought together by common aims. And that means communication, person-to-person, will be crucial to the work. In turn, this implies that we need as much wisdom as we can get about good and effective communication. And that's exactly what this book supplies.

The ways we communicate with each other can spark triumphs or tragedies. Or else, and far too often, they can fall short of sparking much of anything. My friend Jack Malcolm has written this book to bring us the full range of insight we need in order to communicate effectively and well. It's a master class in powerful messaging. I would even say that it's wise, funny, full of great examples, and sprinkled liberally with judicious quotes that both help make a point and remind us of how long we as human beings have been reflecting on these issues. The great thinkers of the past were right about a lot of things. And one of the things they agreed on is this: There is an art to communicating well. And if those philosophers had lived in our time rather than their own, I think they would also agree that Jack is himself a great artist in teaching the art of communicating well, expertly and adroitly showing us the way.

I feel very lucky to know Jack. We often have zoom sessions where we talk over life and work and ideas. He shares with me what he's reading and I return the favor. I'm always impressed with his perspective, as well as how much he knows. As a philosopher myself, who has worked to bring new insight into the world of business for over thirty years, speaking at more than twelve hundred events and authoring over thirty books, I've come to appreciate how rare it is to come across a great communicator and teacher of the art like Jack. In his long career of training sales people to accomplish great things, he understands what it takes to be both informative and persuasive. He draws deep on the wisdom of the past and brings us in this book his own keen realizations of what's needed in our time.

Perhaps the most famous piece of American political rhetoric is Abraham Lincoln's short Gettysburg Address. Moses came down the mountainside and brought his people The Ten Commandments, not Three Hundred and Forty Seven Rules for Proper Living. Jesus later famously summed up those ten in two. President John F. Kennedy is remembered for his concise and pithy statements. Jack Malcolm teaches us that effective communication is lean. Done right, less is more. Everyone's busy. The world is full of demands and distractions. Time is precious. We all need to learn to communicate in ways that take all this into consideration. As a graduate student in philosophy, I remember once hearing someone say of a famous German philosopher that when he got interested in a topic, he always wrote three volumes about the issue. It took the first tome, usually of over three hundred pages, for him to just clear his throat. In book two, he defined the issue, and in volume three he finally told us what he thought. Jack shows us how not to do our own versions of that. And he does so masterfully.

Lean communication doesn't mean that your talk or memo or proposal has to always be short enough so that you could print it out and fit it onto a bumper sticker or the front of a t-shirt. Martin Luther King, Jr. had a dream, and his speech about it changed the world. It wasn't a brief single paragraph. But it was lean and vivid and moving with its power. We want to inform people and convince them and move them to action. And to do so well, we have to be lean communicators who learn to follow the path that this book paves for us.

The rarest focus in our time, and ironically the endeavor that can most powerfully set individuals and organizations apart in excellence and positive effectiveness is the personal and organizational "wisdom work" they do to dig deep, think big, and root everything in the fertile soil of real insight. I'm pleased to have this book on what Jack Malcolm properly calls "lean communication" included in my own publishing imprint of new titles that will, in a variety of ways, help with that work in our day. There is nothing more powerful than the right wisdom at the right time, put into action in all the right ways. I hope you will enjoy this book as much as I have, and that you will also see great results as you put its wisdom to work.

Introduction

It's much easier to follow someone on a long journey if you know your destination and the general route you'll take. That's why this book *begins* with a call to action and a summary: it tells you right away *what* is being asked of you and *why*, followed by a concise summary to help you orient to the ideas that follow.

Call to Action
Embrace the mindset and practices of lean communication to produce better outcomes and relationships, at less cost in time and effort. Talk less, say more.

Summary
*As a knowledge worker, your job is to produce and communicate information and ideas that influence decisions and drive action. But the "customers" for your product are awash in far more information than they can usefully process, so your contribution depends on delivering maximum value with minimum waste. Lean communication provides the principles and skills to enable you to **add value**, **briefly** and **clearly**, and use effective **dialogue** to co-create value with others.*

Using Lean Communication, you will communicate less but better¹, and you will improve your listeners' Return on Time and Effort.

Why Do You Communicate?

You're a knowledge worker, which means that your job is to produce an intangible but useful and valuable product called knowledge. You produce that knowledge in that complex and busy factory called your mind. Just as a factory does, your mind takes in raw materials, applies various forms of work to them, and generates a product. That product comprises information and insights that others can use to make better decisions and take beneficial action to improve outcomes.

Like any other factory, you're measured partly by the quantity, but mostly by the quality of your output—and that requires three key skills: learning, thinking and communicating. Some people are great at learning and/or thinking, but are not so effective at communicating with others; that's a shame because in most circumstances, communication is the most critical of the three skills.

There are two reasons for this. First, to communicate well, you must also do the other two skills well. While you can learn and you can think without communicating, you can't communicate anything of value without first learning or thinking. That's why the discipline of improving the value of your communication will perforce make you a better learner and thinker as well!

The second reason is that, because you have to get things done through others, your most brilliant ideas or insightful recommendations are useless until others hear them, understand them, and act on them. To get anything done in the world, in your enterprise or within your team, you must communicate with others effectively.

To illustrate how critical effective communication is, I recommend an eloquent essay written years ago called "I, Pencil"[2], by economist Leonard Reed. Reed makes the point (no pun intended) that there is no one person in the world who knows how to make from scratch something so simple as a pencil. In the pencil factory, someone operates a machine that someone else built, to cut and shape the cedar that came from someone else, and attaches to it a piece of rubber that came from another country and was produced by chemical processes that someone thought of long ago, and so on.

Most of what you know came from someone else. Most of what you eat, wear, and use came from someone else, and they in turn relied on others to provide the materials and knowledge that enabled them to produce their own small contribution. Life as we know it in a modern society would be impossible without effective communication.

In fact, communicating is by far the most important thing you do; it comprises 80% or more of your time and effort[3]. When you take stock of the time you spend reading and writing emails, searching for information you need, attending meetings, speaking with colleagues, customers and suppliers, delivering and listening to presentations, it's actually a wonder that you have time to do anything *but* communicate.

What's the purpose of all that communication? Quite simply, it's to produce outcomes and maintain relationships. Your purpose is to:
a) **transmit useful information** to
b) **influence decisions** and
c) **drive actions** that
d) **produce favorable outcomes**
e) while maintaining amicable and **productive relationships**.

So it stands to reason that the effectiveness and efficiency of your communication is crucial to your ability to add value to others and to your organization. And because you most likely have a vested interest in increasing your influence and contribution within your organization and your peer group, it's a crucial factor in your personal success as well.

So What's the Problem?

Information is the lifeblood of an organization, and the good news is that in a world where we can transmit huge volumes of information instantly, talk to multiple people around the globe simultaneously, share screens, and exchange clips of cute cats with childhood chums, communication is easier than it's ever been.

Precisely *because* talk is so cheap, fast and ubiquitous, *useful* and *meaningful* communication is at the same time harder than it's ever been. That's because the very ease of creating and transmitting it means that useless information is churned out much faster than ever, and it becomes much tougher to get exactly what you need to make good decisions or take the right action.

Remember the old story of the young boy who received a pile of horse manure, and dove in excitedly because he knew there was a pony in there somewhere? Like that boy, I am an optimist: I do believe the pony *is* in there, but it's getting harder and harder to find because the mountain of crap just keeps getting higher.

That's because, while there's more and more communication, one thing has not changed: our minds still work at the same pace as they have for eons. It still takes us the same amount of time to hear or read what the other person is telling us, assimilate that information into our minds through our working memory, think carefully about it, and use it to form conclusions and make good decisions. All the while, the pace of change means that we are having to make more decisions, faster.

Winning in the Attention Marketplace

We've all heard that time is money, but I would submit that it's more precise to say that attention is money. Getting time on a busy person's calendar is hard enough, but getting their full engagement during that time is much harder; the temptation to multitask, to glance at their email or to be distracted by more pressing concerns, is tough to overcome.

You can't influence if you don't get heard, so if you want to make a bigger difference within an organization or even in your personal relationships, the most important currency you can have is the undivided attention of your audience—and they won't give it to you without begrudging every single second of time and cognitive effort.

With all the world's information seemingly at our fingertips, and with the crazy and ever-growing demands on our time, attention is one of the scarcest resources we have. As economist Herbert Simon said, "What information consumes is rather obvious: it consumes the attention of its recipients. Hence a wealth of information creates a poverty of attention."[4]

To cite two symptomatic examples:

- In 1968, the average length of a political soundbite on national news was 43 seconds. By 1988, it was down to 10 seconds and shrank to 7.3 seconds in 2000, although it has since ticked slightly upwards from there.[5]
- We all know that doctors are under heavy time pressure, but it's still disturbing to know that the average length of time that a doctor will listen to a patient before interrupting is only 18 seconds, according to one study.[6]

Most people nowadays go through life in a state of what writer and consultant Linda Stone calls continuous partial attention[7], where they are constantly scanning their environment for more information, stimulus or novelty. (So far, in writing this section, I have already checked my email twice, refilled my coffee twice, checked the weather and the Wimbledon TV schedule, and answered the phone once.)

So how do you compete in what some call the Attention Economy?[8] One word: *quality*. When quantity is unlimited, quality is more important than ever. In this buzzing confusion, your only hope of capturing and sustaining attention is to deliver maximum value for minimum time and effort. Or to put it another way, you can either increase the payoff from attention, or reduce the cost. If you can do both at once, so much the better.

The Solution is Lean Communication

All of this takes hard, sustained effort on your part, but the investment will definitely pay off for you in the long run. There used to be a brokerage house with the slogan, "When E.F. Hutton talks, people listen." Their commercials always showed two people be speaking in a crowded venue such as a restaurant. The first guy says: "My broker is E.F. Hutton, and E. F. Hutton says…", at which point everyone around them would drop what they were doing and listen expectantly. As you build a reputation for delivering value, it probably won't be so dramatic, but you will be more like the E.F. Hutton commercial: when you talk, people will listen.

Because it's harder than ever to filter out the grain from the chaff, we prize those rare individuals who can give us exactly what we need, when we need it, without wasting our time or making us work too hard to grasp it. Those are the people who get—and deserve—our full attention.

If we prize people who give us value in exchange for our attention, why not strive to do the same for others? Have you ever had the experience of having someone hang on your every word, giving you their full attention in a sincere effort to profit from what you're saying? Feels great, doesn't it?

But how often does that happen?

My goal in writing this book is to help you become one of those rare individuals who command instant and complete attention, by getting you to adopt a mindset of lean communication, and learn and practice its techniques. I hope you'll adopt the mindset immediately; the techniques will take time and effort.

You will learn to give people what they need, when they need it, without wasting their time or making them work too hard. In return for the effort, you will become more effective in your work, more influential, more credible—maybe even more popular!

WHAT is Lean Communication?

Lean communication is modeled on the principles of lean manufacturing, which is both a philosophy and a discipline designed to produce maximum value with minimum waste—to *do more with less.* It was first developed and used by Toyota to achieve unprecedented improvements in production and quality, and has since permeated industry and even service organizations.

In manufacturing, a factory takes in inputs such as metal, ingredients, or components, applies work to them such as bending, cutting, shaping, mixing and assembling, and produces a product that the customer values.

Value is the principal aim in lean: meet the customer's needs, at the right price, and at the right time. Value is paramount. It bears repeating, because the first thing most people think of when they hear "lean" is reducing waste. And it's important to reduce waste, but unless you deliver value, it does not matter how efficiently you do it.

Value is defined by the ultimate customer. Only the customer gets to decide if they received value from the product, so manufacturers pay close attention to the "voice of the customer" to ensure they are meeting their needs. And the customer wants to pay only for value received; they would prefer not to pay for anything that the manufacturer does from start to finish, that does not directly contribute to value, such as defects, overproduction, unnecessary steps, extra features they don't need, and so on.

The Birth of Lean Communication

In 2015, I received a request from the CEO of a large manufacturing company to improve the communication skills of his senior staff—specifically to stop "wasting his time" with long, meandering presentations that seemed designed more to make themselves look good than to transmit useful information.

Every client is different, so whenever I engage with a new client, I strive to present my ideas in ways that resonate with them. Fortunately, although I've never had formal training in lean thinking (and I certainly don't hold myself out as an expert), I've long been fascinated by the idea and had actually read probably a dozen books on the topic, beginning way back in the 1990s with the book: *The Machine That Changed the World*, by James P. Womack, Daniel Roos, and Daniel T. Jones. Because this client was a manufacturing company, I thought they would "get it" quicker if I used the lean manufacturing approach.

It was a bit risky, because it forced me to completely revamp my material, and the more I dug into it, the more I knew I had to learn. But I took on the challenge and it was smashing success. That first session was my "minimum viable product" and since then I've taught the class many times at multiple clients and have continued to refresh and refine the material. This book represents my best possible thinking on it today, but as with any product, it can always be made more valuable to the customer.

The key insight that led to this book is that communication is a process that is very similar to manufacturing a product: the communicator takes in inputs, applies work to them, and produces a "message" that the listener values. The principal difference between the two is that communication, especially dialogue, incorporates the "voice of the customer" real-time, allowing for the co-creation of value.

We'll begin by defining value and waste in communication terms.

Value is defined as:
effective communication
that improves personal and/or business outcomes
while respecting the relationship

You know you have created value when one or more of the following things happen:

- The communication is effective: the other person received the message as you intended.
- The other person is better equipped to make a decision or take action that improves their personal situation, and/or:
- The organization is better off, or a higher purpose than individual gain is served.
- The other person feels good about the communication because the relationship is respected.

Waste is defined simply as:
any work or input that does not directly contribute to value

In manufacturing, there is a lot of waste. The actual time spent performing the tasks to produce the final product is usually less than 10% of the total time from start to finish, and fewer than 30% of those tasks add value from the customer's perspective. For example, the end customer doesn't care that you had to move work-in-process from one station to another. To the customer, that's just waste that they don't want to pay for.

It's tough to find similar statistics for communication, but the following passage from the book, *Simplicity*, is instructive:

"About 80 percent of your internal communication—meetings, teleconferences, presentations, emails, etc.—consists of

- *Sharing information that does not require action, and/or*
- *Communicating something for which there is no discernible consequence if the recipient ignores it"⁹*

If the message can be ignored with no discernible consequences, that's clearly wasted breath, ink or pixels!

It's easy to see and hear the waste in communication all around us. Everyday examples include sitting through long and unproductive meetings waiting your turn to speak for a minute or two, hoping for someone to get to the point, trying to decipher vague explanations, receiving incorrect information, fancy slides that show more pride in design than content, and so on. This list could easily continue, but that would probably be wasteful.

More poetically, perhaps, Konrad Lorenz put it this way:
What is thought is not said
What is said is not heard
What is heard is not understood
What is understood is not believed
What is believed is not yet advocated
What is advocated is not yet acted on
What is acted on is not yet completed

Ponder that for a minute: does it resonate with you? When I show this quote in my classes, there is instant and probably unanimous agreement that this describes their work situation. [10]

All that waste in communication is enormously costly. The most obvious impact is the sheer amount of wasted time. While it's probably impossible to measure the actual cost, here are a few data points that can illuminate the scope of the problem:

Meetings: One of the most obvious culprits is meetings. A study conducted by Bain and Company analyzed the Outlook schedules of everyone in a large company to figure out the actual impact of the company's weekly Executive Committee Status meeting.

- To prepare for the meeting, senior-level participants would meet with their unit heads. **7,000 hours**
- Unit heads meet with their senior advisers to prepare for those meetings: **11 unit heads x 1,800 hours = 20,000 hours**
- Senior advisers get information from their teams: **21 team meetings averaging 3,000 hours = 63,000 hours**
- The teams need to spend time in prep meetings synthesizing the information: **130 meetings x 1,500 hours = 195,000 hours**

No wonder John Kenneth Galbraith said, "*Meetings are indispensable when you don't want to do anything.*"[11]

Email: The next largest chunk of time taken out of your day is dealing with email, which takes up about 28% of your time according to a survey by McKinsey.[12] Another study calculated that the average worker receives 124 emails a day.[13] Assuming that 80% of communication can be ignored without consequence, that's 100 emails a day worth of waste.

Reading and writing: Josh Bernoff, the author of *Writing Without Bullshit*, says that employees spend 22% of their time reading, and because so much of it is poorly written, "America is spending 6 percent of total wages on time wasted attempting to get meaning out of poorly written material"[14]. What does 6% of your company's wages amount to?

While time wasted may be easier to measure, the cost of errors due to misunderstanding can be even higher. In fact, the airline industry has created a complete training program called crew resource management in response to several fatal crashes that were traced to faulty communication in the cockpit; in 1999, the $125 million Mars Climate Orbiter mission failed because Lockheed Martin engineers used English units in navigation information and handed it off to NASA, which assumed they were metric units. No doubt you have experienced numerous instances of misunderstanding in your business life as well, some of which may have been quite costly, at least personally if not financially.

Let's not forget the psychic cost in the form of frustration that people can feel when they impatiently wait for someone to get to the point, or have to sift through a lot of buzzwords and bloviation to uncover what the speaker is trying to say, or see no value in a conversation. In fact, that frustration was probably the main feeling that drove my first Lean Communication client to ask me to create a course for his company.

What's less obvious but probably more important is that all of these forms of waste interfere with the ability to devote enough time and attention to think deeply and carefully about important issues. For example, have you ever been in a meeting that wasted a lot of time on irrelevant information, so that when the time comes to wrap things up and make a decision, the decision feels rushed, or based on superficial information?

As Lorenz described it, there are seven steps possible between thought and action, between ideas and results—seven opportunities to either make a positive contribution or to waste the opportunity. Imagine the payoff to you and your organization if you could attack and improve every one of those seven steps, and that is precisely what you will be equipped to do if you adopt the mindset, learn the elements, and practice the skills of lean communication.

Let's take a deeper look at what it will personally mean to you and your listeners when you practice lean communication.

The Personal Economics of Lean Communication

In a free market, companies create profits for themselves by creating value that others are willing to pay for, in excess of their costs of production. If they want to generate more profits, they must either increase the value and/or reduce their costs, and this focus on the bottom-line forces a customer-centered discipline, because only the customer can decide if they are delivering value at an acceptable cost. Before introducing a new product, they have to think carefully about whether customers will buy it, and whether they can produce it profitably.

To help themselves in this quest, many companies have adopted lean production as a framework for constantly looking for ways to maximize value and minimize waste. (Not all costs are waste; for example, the cost of the metal that goes into the product is unavoidable. What might be avoidable is the waste of rejected material, or putting more into the product than the customer actually needs, or losing a portion to scrap, etc.)

When their customers consider whether to buy their products, they measure the value they receive in terms of ROI, which simply is a division problem, with **Return** on top and **Investment** on the bottom. While there is always a lot of gray area in deciding what results and costs to include in the calculation, it's still a reasonably straightforward way of prioritizing how to invest their limited capital.

We all take this for granted when it comes to business, but is it possible that we forget it when we communicate? Just as companies don't pump out products unless they think they'll sell, we should not just pump out words without thinking about whether they are worth listening to. Will listeners be willing to pay the price in time and effort to hear what you have to say?

Return on Time and Effort

Of course, listeners don't actually calculate the ROI of speaking with you. Or do they? They actually do in a way, albeit not that overtly.

It's extremely slippery to pin down a quantifiable return on communication, but we can at least try to measure the unmeasurable by applying the same thought process as ROI. Let's call it **RoTE**, or **Return on Time and Effort**:

$$\frac{\textbf{Return}}{\textbf{Time x Effort}}$$

Return: What value does your audience receive from listening to you? We measure value in lean communication in terms of outcomes and relationships. When the information shared improves a decision or leads to effective action that generates measurable outcomes, you could theoretically put an actual dollar value on that conversation or presentation. In reality it's not that simple, especially since most important decisions usually require a series of conversations, presentations, and messages going back and forth. But just because value can't be measured precisely doesn't mean people don't know it when they see it, which is why value is defined by the listener, not the speaker.

Practically and mathematically, **R** is the most important factor in the equation. If it's zero or negative, no amount of brevity or clarity will make the communication worthwhile, and if it's high enough, almost any amount of time and effort will be worth devoting to it.

That said, it's still important to concentrate on the denominator of the equation. Unlike ROI, in which the investment is only calculated in dollars, communication requires the investment of two costly currencies: time and cognitive effort.

Time is of course the most easily measurable factor. How much time do you take in getting your message across? Do you get right to the point, or do you overload your listeners with information they already know; do you hold back vital information out of fear of offending; do you have trouble resisting interesting but irrelevant snippets and trivia; do you have to reexplain or clarify your meaning?

The paradox of brevity is that you as a communicator need to invest your time to save time for your audience. When Mark Twain received this telegram from a publisher:

NEED 2-PAGE SHORT STORY TWO DAYS.

He sent back this reply:

NO CAN DO 2 PAGES TWO DAYS. CAN DO 30 PAGES
2 DAYS. NEED 30 DAYS TO DO 2 PAGES.

So, there is a cost/benefit analysis you have to run through your mind: is there any net value added when you invest your own time to save time for the listener? The answer is almost always yes. First, because when you are presenting to audiences of more than one person, it's easy to see that an extra hour of preparation to shorten your presentation can pay off in multiples, especially when you are presenting to higher-level people whose opportunity cost of listening can quickly add up to big numbers. Second, the effort of making things brief also affects the R and the E of the equation. It affects Return by sharpening your thinking, and effort by making it easier for listeners to understand.

Effort is harder to measure but no less important than time. The simple truth is that thinking is hard work, and we generally avoid doing any more than is absolutely necessary. As with brevity, you work hard so your listeners don't have to. The harder you make people work to understand what you're saying, the more of their time you take and the less value you add to them. In the worst case, if they find it too hard to understand you, they will give up—and that's wasteful for all parties.

By making it easy for them to understand, you also do yourself a favor, because they will be much more likely to repay you by being open to your message and accepting your logic. As renowned psychologist Daniel Kahneman says, in the recipient's mind, simple = true.[15]

Building equity
When companies produce value in excess of cost they generate

profits, which in turn builds equity that strengthens their balance sheets and provides resources to generate future profits. It's the same way with personal communication. As you build a reputation for delivering good value through lean communication, you are accruing personal equity in the form of credibility.

Any increase in personal credibility is useful, especially because at some point it may even lead to the Matthew Effect[16], where the rich get richer, as initial advantages accumulate and build on themselves. By consistently delivering a high RoTE, you will generate greater trust with more decision makers who will require less verification of your arguments and facts and save time over the long run—for yourself and for others.

That can create a virtuous circle of influence that can power your career as long as you tend it carefully. People with a reputation for being lean communicators (even if others don't recognize the term) tend to get their emails read and their calls returned. That is priceless, whether you can put a dollar value on it or not.

And if you don't think that's a strong enough reason to jealously guard your personal credibility, remember that the Matthew Effect also works in reverse: the poor get poorer. If others don't perceive much value from communicating with you, they pay less and less attention, until you sink slowly into irrelevance.

What Does Lean Communication Look Like?

What are the principles and skills that will make you a lean communicator? This figure captures all the important elements of lean communication and will serve as our agenda and overview for this entire book. In fact, I will take a page and a half right here to summarize the entire lean communication approach.

Lean Communication in Brief

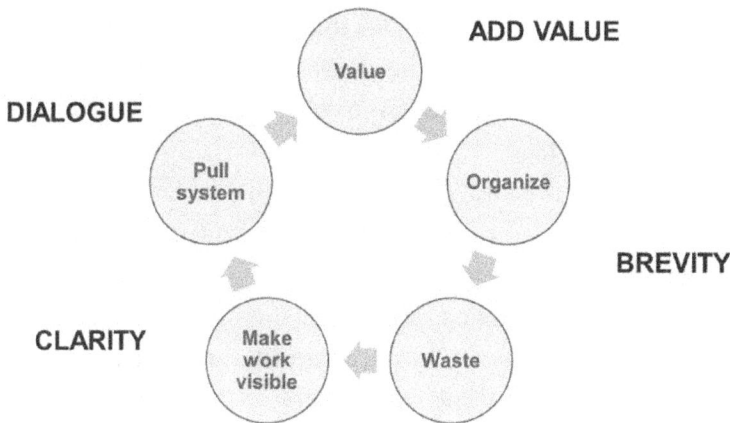

Value: Above all, communication must produce value; this is the one indispensable element of the five. There are two tools to ensure that you deliver maximum value. Because value is defined by the listener, the first tool is *Make it about Them,* which simply means fitting your message to the audience by taking their perspective and addressing what they care about. The second is *Have a Clear Purpose* by answering the Question, which is always in their minds when you approach: "What do you want me to do and why should I do it?"

Organize: Organize means to arrange your message for maximum logic and clarity, and that typically means you express your ideas differently from the way you arrived at them. The best form of organization to reduce both the time and effort it takes for the other person to understand is *top-down,* or bottom-line-up-front.

Waste: Next, we will consider how to identify and therefore cut out the clutter of information that hides our true message. *SO WHAT?* is the filter we use; another way to say is what is their Need to Know this, and what does it mean to them?

Making work visible: Making work visible means that you make it easier for other people to follow your logic and understand your explanations if you make your thinking as transparent as possible. First, you show them the *structure of your thinking*, speak with *candor and the appropriate level of directness*, and employ *"user-friendly" language.*

Pull System: The ideal lean message will deliver just the information the listener needs, when they need it. But since everyone starts with a different level of understanding, processes information at different speeds, and needs their own specific information for their purposes, you can only accomplish this by using the *pull system*. This means that you must use *lean questioning* and *lean listening* to make adjustments along the way.

Ten Keys of Lean Communication

These five principles are the mechanism by which we apply the time-tested techniques of lean thinking to communication, but to apply them in your daily work, it makes more sense to distill them down to ten practical skills, arranged for convenience into ABCD.

Add Value
1. Make It about Them
2. Answer the Question (ATQ)

Brevity
3. Top-down Communication
4. So What Filter

Clarity
5. Transparent Logic
6. Candor and Directness
7. User-Friendly Language

Dialogue
8. Just-in-time Communication
9. Lean Questioning
10. Lean Listening

Are there Limits to Lean Communication?

Before we go any further, it's important to stress that Lean Communication is a tool kit, and you should always use the appropriate tool for the right job—it's not the only way you should be communicating.

For example, I like to say that you should not try this at home! Seriously, the point is that when the relationship is more important than the factual exchange of information, lean communication is not always the best way to communicate.

You may also need to dispense with lean communication when the situation calls for divergent thinking, such as when brainstorming solutions to a problem. You can use it to define the problem, and then later on to converge on a decision, but not during the middle stages when you want to encourage a free-flowing exchange of ideas.

Finally, you should be sensitive to the culture in which you are using it. Western culture generally encourages direct, context-free communication, while other cultures may find that uncomfortable or even rude.

As you get comfortable with the skills and practices, you will be able to use your own judgment to know when to communicate lean and when not to.

Mindset and Practices

By now I hope you have a deeper appreciation for why you and your organization need lean communication. By simply having a different mindset—the *humility* to recognize that you need to change, first of all; taking *personal responsibility* to add value in all your communications, and the *kaizen* spirit to constantly look for ways to improve and root out waste—you've made an excellent start.

In the rest of this book, you will receive the tools and sharpen the skills that will make you a rare and valued lean communicator. Webster's Dictionary contains 19 definitions of the word *practice*, but the first three are especially relevant here:

1. habitual or customary performance
2. habit; custom
3. repeated performance or systematic exercise for the purpose of acquiring skill or proficiency

If you learn the ten keys of lean communication in the pages that follow, practice them repeatedly until they become habits, you will surely acquire the skill to elevate your customary performance of communication.

Note:
As you read this book, you will encounter sections in gray, such as this one. I've marked them this way because they are "interesting", which means that technically they violate the Four-I Test.[17] But, to the extent that they keep your attention, illustrate real-world applications, or make some ideas easier to remember, they can add value.

If you want to take the strictest interpretation of lean and classify this as waste, you can simply skip the gray sections.

A

Add Value

If you're manufacturing a product, the only way to add value to customers is to find a need and fill it.

By analogy, the first and most important rule of lean communication is that you must have something worthwhile to say. Remember the old advice about not saying anything unless you can improve on silence? You improve on silence by saying something useful, something that they can use to improve personal and/or business outcomes.

In effect, you deliver a message that fills a need. That is the only path to value.

Value for whom? The first imperative is that you must add value to the intended recipient—the listener decides if what you said or wrote is valuable to them. But this is not a recipe for total altruism or for being a doormat— just as a company is entitled to a profit from delivering products to customers, you are also perfectly entitled to add value to yourself and defend your own interests. It's not "either/or", it's "both, and...".

Value is the starting point of lean communication; it's the "R" in RoTE. Simple math shows that you can't have a return without a positive number in the numerator, no matter how quick or easy you make it for the other person, which is why value is absolutely the most critical of the five principles of lean communication. Without it, you have nothing. With it, listeners will put up with a lot of waste as long as they get value from their investment.

At the risk of repetition, let's revisit the definition of value and dig into it a little deeper. You will recall from the introduction that communication value is defined as:

> *"effective communication*
> *that improves business and/or personal outcomes*
> *while respecting the relationship."*

Let's break this definition down into its parts:

Communication must be effective. Did they get it? The first point about adding value is that your message must get through; transmission is useless without reception, and just saying or writing something does not mean the other person got it. As George Bernard Shaw said, "The single biggest problem in communication is the illusion that it has taken place." You must take responsibility for ensuring the message has been received as you intended it. When what is said is not heard, or what's heard has not been understood as you meant it, your communication has not been effective.

Nothing happens unless the other party gets it as you intended it. This implies a responsibility on your part: you can't control whether the listener will act as you intend, but you *can* control whether they hear and understand your message.

It must improve business and/or personal outcomes. Lean communication is a tool to get things done, to improve outcomes for others by enabling and supporting better-informed decisions or action.

Whose outcomes are we talking about? When you communicate with someone in a business context, there are three possible parties that could benefit from the message: you, the listener, and the organization or task. Ideally, all three would benefit, but of course that's not always possible. But two out of three is pretty good. Sometimes you need to convince the other person to do something not because they're going to like it or personally benefit from it, but because it's for the good of the organization. You *can* succeed occasionally when you communicate to get something that will only benefit yourself, but that's not a sound approach in the long run.

It must respect the relationship. Henry Ford once said that it was unfortunate that every time he hired a hand, a head came with it. Tellingly, he neglected to add "heart" to that statement, betraying an outdated and yet still-too-prevalent attitude that views others instrumentally, or solely as means to an end; it is the complete antithesis of what we mean by preserving the relationship. Regardless of how important the decision or action is, don't to get so focused on the outcome you want in the conversation that you neglect the people side of it. It may sound obvious, but at least in my case, it took years for the message to fully sink in!

This is not a license to hide or sugarcoat things that may need to be said. There are times when the situation calls for harsh truths that the other person may not want to hear, but you might have to say something for the good of the larger picture.

But even in these situations you should always strive to respect the individual and preserve or enhance the relationship. Besides being the right thing to do, it's also effective, for two reasons. First, unless your communications are purely transactional, where you will never see that person again, everything you do in a communication will influence the effectiveness of future conversations. Second, that's a human being on the other end of your communication process, and respect, liking and trust are much more likely to foster engagement and willing participation.

Depending on the importance of the end goal, sometimes the relationship has to take a backseat to the expected outcome. Sometimes it's the other way around. So, unfortunately there is not a clear-cut consistent rule to recommend, other than to use your best judgment and maintain an attitude of respect.

But in the end, companies are not social clubs, so think of outcomes as integral to value and relationships as important.

Answering **The Question**

There is another way to view value that may also clarify the concept: did you answer their question?

In keeping with our lean manufacturing analogy, it's useful to think of the end "product" of our communication as the answer to a fundamental question in the listener's mind. Answering the question means two different things, depending on who is driving the conversation. In the questioner-led scenario, the other person is driving the exchange by asking you questions.

In that scenario, the question is simply the one they asked. In questioner-led communications, the other person probably has a good reason for asking their question, so we'll assume the answer will improve their situation in some way. We consider lean ways to answer direct questions in Chapter 8.

But what if you're the one bringing up the topic or starting the conversation? In this speaker-led scenario, you initiate the conversation for your own reasons, whether you're sending them an email, popping into their office to talk, or making a formal presentation to a group. They may appreciate the banter, or the interesting story about your weekend, or some fascinating bit of trivia you share, but ultimately their test of value is whether you answered the question that is on their minds.

To see what the question is, let's switch sides for a minute and pretend you're sitting at your desk, hard at work and pressed for time, and a subordinate enters and asks, "Got a minute?" What would be your first thought?

Probably, some variation of "What does he want?" If he gets right to the point, you may not like it, but at least the tension of not knowing what he's going to ask goes away. But if he meanders around the shrubbery you'll start getting impatient and maybe even a little suspicious. You start wondering when the other shoe is going to drop.

When you finally grasp what they want you to decide or do, the next obvious thought is "Why?", or slightly more elaborately, "What's in it for me?" Of course, since you're totally focused on the bigger picture and being a team player, you might also think, "What's in it for us?"

Returning to the scenario where you are initiating the conversation, your communication would take a huge step toward lean and practically guarantee that you improve on silence, if every time you stepped into someone's office to speak to them, or every time you sat down to write an email, you saw a sign that read:

"__What__ do you want me to do and __why__?"

Those two questions, *what* and *why*, must be answered for communication to add value, because the purpose of communication inside an organization is to enable, facilitate, or improve on decisions or action. If you don't ask for a decision or action, what's the point of the conversation?

Even if you are "just sharing information", there must be a reason you want them to know the information shared, even if the only action you want is: "Don't do anything; it's all under control." In this scenario, a variation of the question is:

"__What__ do you want me to know, and __why__ should I care?"

What and *why* are the end goals of your communication, so why not start with your goals clearly in mind? If you know those are the questions they will have in mind when you initiate the conversation, do them—and yourself—a favor by having an unambiguous answer for them.

When you have a clear and compelling answer to the question, it can save a lot of time and effort on the part of both parties. One of my clients moved to a new company, where he faced the challenge of needing to add headcount in a difficult economy. He told the head of HR: "I need to hire an account manager to support $500 million in revenue from (a new account)." He received instant approval without a question being asked. Imagine what that did for his credibility going forward!

Answering the question forces you to focus on the purpose of your message, framed in terms of benefit to the ultimate customer—either the listener personally or the task/organization. If you don't have a good reason for them to hear it, why are you saying it? Your answer to that question has to be defined in terms of something that is good for the other person or something that they value. There are many ways the listener can benefit, and we cover those in more detail in just a few pages.

Answering the question gives you your headline, and it needs to be crystal-clear—in their mind as well as yours. I have seen so many times in presentations classes, for example, where people can't answer this question about presentations *they have already prepared*. They have a mass of words and pile of slides, and they can't sum it up to one key message. When I force them to start from the beginning, the discipline of thinking through their key message first helps the rest of the message fall into place. As the Roman orator, Cato, said, "Grasp the subject, the words will follow."

The corollary to the rule that you must have something worthwhile to say, is that when you don't have anything worthwhile to say, keep quiet.

When General Ira Eaker led the first contingents of the 8th Air Force to England in 1942, hopes were running high for America to add its muscle to the war against Nazi Germany. So, when he was asked to speak at a luncheon, the audience was poised to hang on his every word. Here's his entire speech:

"We won't do much talking until we've done more fighting. After we've gone, we hope you'll be glad we came."

He sat down amid thunderous applause.

How will you know if you added value?

Value is paramount. As we go through the five elements of lean communication, you will see that there are plenty of instances when it might make sense to violate one or more of the elements—but *never* value. It is not only the starting point but also absolutely the most important of the five elements. Being only slightly facetious, value is the pony in the pile of manure.

Proceeding directly from our definition, we can see that it's actually quite simple: this very short checklist captures everything you need to do to ensure that you add value in every conversation or communication with another person:

☐ Did you improve the situation or outcome?
☐ Did you respect the relationship?
☐ Did you answer the question they asked?

As long as you have checked at least one of the boxes, you have added value. If you can check more than one, so much the better.

Of course, as with anything "simple", the devil is in the details. *What* to do is simple, *how* to do it is the subject of the next two chapters, which together comprise the first two principles of lean communication:

1. Make it about them
2. Have a clear purpose

1

Lean Communication Key #1:
Make It About Them

Call to action

Use outside-in thinking to express your message in terms of what your listeners need and how they understand.

Summary

In lean communication, the listener ultimately defines value, and that is a function of how they can use your message to improve their personal and/or organizational outcomes. The surest way to maximize value is to approach the communication from their perspective, and express your message in terms of what they want and need. This requires outside-in thinking, also known as cognitive empathy, and it's a skill that can be cultivated.

Imagine this situation: you're choosing a wedding present for two close friends. You've visited their registry to get ideas, but you also have an idea for an excellent and unique gift that you are sure they will like. Which would you choose?

If you opted for the unique gift, you're not alone; after all, it's more thoughtful, isn't it? You're also probably wrong. According to one study, recipients of gifts that they had chosen beforehand reported "significantly greater appreciation of the registry gifts than the unique gifts."[1]

The explanation given is that the gift-givers imagined how they would feel if they received those gifts, but they didn't do a very good job of figuring out how the recipients would feel. It was a bit like buying a shirt for someone else because it fits you perfectly.

To cite a personal example, I post a lot of blog articles and videos and I've learned that it's almost impossible to predict how many views I will get for each. I may love a video and think it's a fascinating topic, and I'll get very little reaction, or vice-versa. It's a constant reminder that people do things for their own reasons, not for yours.

Your first priority as a lean communicator is to add value, but only the recipient of the message gets to decide whether they received value, and how much. This makes it crucial to take their perspective to understand how they view, think, and feel about the situation. It's easier said than done, because it requires nothing less than a reversal in your normal habits of thought.

Outside-in thinking

Determining what the listener most values requires *outside-in thinking*. Outside-in thinking recognizes that people do things for their own reasons, not yours, and it forces you to think carefully and deeply about how they define value. It answers the *why* side of the question.

In lean terms, you think about the customer and their needs first, and work backwards from there to produce value that they will pay for. It's exactly the same thing in lean communication, where you start from the perspective of the ultimate listener and work backwards to properly frame your communication. You may have a lot of things that you think should be said, but the ultimate customer is the sole judge of value, so when answering the *why* question, you'll save a lot of time and effort by understanding their needs first.

The fact that people do things for their own reasons and not for yours may sound blindingly obvious, but it's so easily and often overlooked. When I work with coaching clients to help them become more effective communicators, they often ask me how to sell an idea internally, perhaps to their boss or to another group within the company whose cooperation they need. My first question is always, "What's in it for them to agree?" Almost invariably—after a long pause—the answer comes back, "I haven't thought about it that way." That's because people are so focused on their own reasons for doing things that they neglect the reasons that matter to the people who control whether those things get done.

Look at it as the difference between a pharmacist and a doctor. Who knows more about that pill you take, the pharmacist or the doctor? Clearly the pharmacist does; she can tell you all about the chemical makeup, recommended dosages, side effects, etc. So why don't you go straight to the pharmacist when you're ailing? Because the doctor knows much more about *you*. The doctor asks questions and diagnoses before writing the prescription.

This pharmacist approach is all too common in business, as many firms rely on the better mousetrap theory, constantly striving to produce better, more efficient and more elegant products—many of which either don't sell or develop over time into complex, over-engineered "solutions" that are difficult to use and often create more problems than they solve. Is it any wonder that, according to the late Harvard professor Clayton Christensen, up to 95% of new product introductions fail?[2]

The pharmacist approach is also far too common in communication; we try to sell the solutions and ideas we have because they are the ones we know and understand. When we run into resistance, we push harder by polishing and "improving" what we know instead of starting fresh from the point of view of the listener.

Why does that happen? We all have two qualities that make it difficult to start from the listener's perspective first: we're selfish and we're lazy. Those are not value judgments—they're objective facts. We're selfish in the sense that we see the world mostly from our own perspective, and we try to further our own goals and desires. Figuratively, the world *does* revolve around us, and we all go through life mostly using inside-out thinking, viewing the world through the lens of our own needs and desires. It's perfectly natural, and it's easy. It's our default mode: we naturally begin with *what* we want before we get to *why* the other person would want to do it.

We're also lazy—or, as psychologists express it more tactfully, we are "cognitive misers." Thinking differently than we normally do requires mental effort that we prefer to avoid if possible. Sometimes it's not laziness so much as it is overconfidence: we think we know more about what others will care about than we actually do. Whatever the reason, it's not easy to think carefully about perspectives other than our own.

But fortunately for our communication, and for our enterprises and our communities, we are also capable—at least in short bursts—of engaging in *outside-in thinking*.

To think outside-in you must start with *why*, by putting yourself in the other's mind and seeing the situation from their perspective and understanding their needs and concerns. If you want to communicate effectively and improve outcomes, you need outside-in thinking because it's not about you—it's about your audience or your listener. You may have the idea and the impeccable logic to support it, but they have what you don't: the power to understand, agree and act. Outside-in thinking will help you explain it in terms they can understand, give them reasons they can agree with, and move them to action.

Outside-in thinking reminds you that you haven't said anything until they've heard, you haven't explained until they've understood, you haven't taught until they've learned, you haven't convinced until they've agreed, and you haven't sold until they've bought.

Outside-in communicators know that the quality of the reception is more important than the elegance of the transmission, so they begin their communication process from the point of view of the other person first.

Inside-out communicators craft messages and create slide decks that are one-size-fits-all. The message and its expression are the same for everyone. Outside-in communicators customize their messages and approach to the preferences and needs of the audience.

Inside-out communicators strive for wins for themselves, even if it means a loss for the other party. Outside-in communicators look for ways to craft win-win solutions that increase the total value for all concerned.

Inside-out communicators worry about sounding smart by making things complicated; outside-in thinkers work hard to simplify and explain to make others smarter. Jennie Jerome, Winston Churchill's mother, gave a great example of this when she compared two of the great British Prime Ministers, saying, "When I sat next to Mr. Gladstone, I thought he was the cleverest man in England. But when I sat next to Mr. Disraeli, I thought I was the cleverest woman."

Inside-out communicators view listeners' objections as obstacles to be overcome in order to get the outcomes they want, and they prefer to avoid them. Outside-in communicators welcome objections, because they provide a window into the other person's needs, and provide information that may be used to work together with the other person to devise even better outcomes.

Here's a table that summarizes some of the major differences in attitude and behaviors between the two ways of thinking:

Inside-out Thinking	Outside-in Thinking
Talking more	Listening more
Transmission	Reception
Message is the same for everyone	Customized message
Product-focused	Customer-focused
Win-lose	Win-win
Shallow focus on positions	Deeper focus on interests
Try to sound smart	Make them feel smart
Natural and easy	A learned skill that requires work
Show how much you know	Tell what they need to know
Trying to be interesting	Be interested
Objections are obstacles	Objections are opportunities
Fits you	Fits them

For a before-and-after example of outside-in thinking, I'm reminded of a presentation one of my students put together for the workshop I was running on internal presentations. He was organizing a presentation to convince the CFO to approve a budget variance in order to purchase new workstations for his veteran engineers. Economic conditions had put the company in a spending freeze, and a request of this sort required special approval.

For his first effort, he justified the need by explaining that newer engineers received new workstations when they came on board, while those with longer tenure were stuck with older models. He said it was causing friction and morale problems, and he wanted to be fair to his more senior staff. I asked him what was the likelihood that the CFO would actually care whether the engineers were happy. He admitted that the probable response would be that everyone has to make sacrifices during this tough period.

I then asked him, what would the CFO care about? After a little brainstorming, he came up with reasoning that the newer workstations would improve productivity of the entire team through their superior performance, which would reduce the risk of delays in launching a new product. The resulting presentation was much more focused on the needs of the person making the decision, and I heard later that the request was approved.

Hiring an accountant

Even accountants benefit from outside-in thinking. A business owner interviewed three candidates for an accounting position, asking each the same question: "What's 2 +2?"

The first candidate replied "Four." He did not get the job.

The next candidate said, "Normally it's four, but depending on how you classify certain things it can be three or five." He was told that they might get back to him.

The third candidate asked, "What do you want it to be?" He was hired on the spot.

Outside-in Thinking Is a Skill

So far we have viewed outside-in thinking as an attitude, but to apply it practically, we also have to see it as a skill. In psychological terms, the skill is known as cognitive empathy or perspective-taking. It's essentially a form of mind-reading, being able to see the situation from the point of view of another person. It's a skill that may be unique to humans, and begins to develop around the time we are three years old and ends only when we attain positions of power.[3]

Most relevant to our purpose of becoming lean communicators is that cognitive empathy can be learned, and can be improved with awareness and practice. For example, Massachusetts General Hospital has devised a training program that has been shown to improve their physicians' perceived empathy.[4] But you don't need a formal training program. You already have the mental tools to think more carefully about the other's perspective, as long as you remember to use them. You just have to cultivate a mindset of curiosity and consideration for the views of others, and remind yourself to think about their perspective until it becomes a habit.

Research has shown that negotiators who can understand and frame their communications from the other person's point of view can get better outcomes for both sides.[5] That's because focusing too closely on your own interests can blind you to ways to create more value by trading something minor that the other person values more highly.

That research applies to communications between two unrelated parties, where only two perspectives matter, yours and theirs. But when you're communicating with someone internally, there is a third perspective that's at least as important as those of the speaker and listener: that of the ultimate "customer." Because you both work for the same organization and at least theoretically align your interests with your employer, the team and/or the task is the ultimate customer who determines value.

So, if outside-in thinking means thinking from the point of view of your listeners, there are actually two perspectives you need to consider, which we will call WIFM and WIFU.

WIFM: WIFM stands for "What's in it for me?" Think of it as the call letters for your listener's favorite radio station: the one that will ensure you get the best reception. You almost always have to produce a favorable personal outcome for the listener, because they, like everyone else, are largely driven by self-interest. They are always asking "what's in it for me?", and you had better have a good answer. Did you provide a personal benefit to the listener? While this does not always apply, ultimately all decisions are personal, so you should strive to frame communications in terms of the other person's benefit.

WIFU: WIFM is important, but it's usually not enough. We also need WIFU, in which the U can stand for either "us", meaning the team, or for the "ultimate customer." Many people will do things for the good of the group they belong to, even when it carries a personal cost to themselves.

Adam Grant and David Hoffman ran an experiment in a hospital that demonstrated this. They posted two different signs near soap dispensers:

Hand hygiene prevents you from catching diseases.

Or,

Hand hygiene prevents patients from catching diseases.

The first sign had no effect at all on hand-washing. The second sign resulted in medical professionals washing 10% more often and using 33% more soap.[6]

By asking about WIFU in addition to WIFM you may be able to tap into higher motivations than simple self-interest. And, even if the other person's *real* motive is self-serving, you can at least give them cover to help them rationalize their decision to others.

In fact, relying only on WIFM can sometimes backfire on you, as illustrated in this story that Chip and Dan Heath tell in their book, *Made to Stick*. A marketer was testing messages to help sell an educational film about fire safety to firefighters. He first asked fire units if they would like to review the film for their educational programs, and their replies were enthusiastically positive. Then, he asked them if they would prefer a popcorn popper or a set of steak knives for reviewing the film. The general response was "Do you think we'd use a fire safety program because of some #*$@! popcorn popper?!"[7]

The problem is that we are often wrong about others' motivations. Clearly, people do consider their own self-interest when they make choices or decisions, but research has shown that we overestimate to what extent. First, consider your own motivations: how often do you consider other factors besides your own self-interest when making a decision, such as whether it's good for the company you work for, or it's just the right thing to do? Next, ask the same question with regard to others.

Chances are, the answer to the second question was much lower than the answer to the first. As to ourselves, we know that our motivations are a mixture of narrow self-interest—extrinsic rewards—and intrinsic rewards such as feeling good about ourselves, doing something worthwhile or meaningful, personal growth, etc. But when we think about others, we overestimate their reliance on "selfish" extrinsic rewards.[8]

Thinking and communicating consistently in terms of the bigger picture can only help your own credibility and influence in the long run. It shows an ownership mentality and an appreciation for the strategic view that others will respect and appreciate. It shows a willingness to put the needs of the group ahead of your own, so if the time ever comes when you do ask for something that only benefits yourself, you are more likely to get a sympathetic hearing.

Besides that, let's be realistic (some would say cynical) for a moment. Even if you and the other person are clearly acting out of pure self-interest, you both know that dressing up the decision in terms of bigger picture reasoning is useful for long-term career success.

How U.S. Grant won a battle with outside-in thinking
Throughout history, great generals have used outside-in thinking to get into the mind of their adversaries and adjust their strategy accordingly. Although "adversary" isn't the way we want to consider those we're trying to persuade, the principle of outside-in thinking is the same.

In February 1862, Grant commanded the Union forces that attacked the neighboring Confederate forts, Henry and Donelson, which guarded the Tennessee and Cumberland Rivers. Fort Henry fell relatively quickly, but Fort Donelson was a tougher nut to crack. It was nominally commanded by John Floyd, but Grant knew that Floyd would defer to the judgment of his second in command, General Gideon Pillow. As Grant later wrote in his memoirs, he knew Pillow from their previous service together in the war against Mexico, and he was confident that he could approach aggressively against him, so he moved his forces as close to the fort as possible.

Knowing they could not hold out for long, on February 15th the Confederates launched a vigorous attack against the Union forces in an attempt to escape the fort. The plan came close to success, but the Union lines just managed to hold on. Fearing Union reprisals, both Floyd and Pillow—establishing a tradition that incompetent CEOs follow to this day—snuck out during the night, leaving Simon Bolivar Buckner to unconditionally surrender the fort.

Buckner, who had served with Grant in California, told him that if he had been in command Grant would not have gotten up close to Donelson as easily as he did. As Grant later said in his memoirs: "I told him that if he had been in command I should not have tried in the way I did."[9]

HOW TO FIGURE OUT WHAT THEY NEED

While emotional empathy primarily deals with wants, cognitive empathy is more about needs, and sometimes there can be a big difference between the two. For example, there may be times the other person will not want to do what they need to do for the good of the organization, or even for their own good.

We all want a lot of things that aren't necessarily what we need; anyone who has children knows the difference between the two. I'm not suggesting that you should take the parent role in communications with others, but you will be more effective if you step back and consider what they need and not just what they want.

In negotiations, it's a little more subtle: it's the difference between the *positions* someone takes and their actual *interests*. For example, in a sales negotiation the buyer insists on a lower price. Price is their position, but their real interest is lower overall costs, or higher profits. That may seem like a purely academic distinction, but if you can show them how paying a higher price will reduce costs in the long run, both sides win.

Of course, understanding their needs takes work on your part. It helps to know as much as possible about both their extrinsic and intrinsic needs.

Extrinsic needs

Extrinsic needs are the most commonly addressed needs in business communication, for the simple reason that they are easier to discover and to talk about. They generally relate to the other's objective goals, the ones that can be and usually are measured, and they're more likely to be publicly known.

To discover and discuss extrinsic needs, you need to know as much as possible about: a) where are they now, b) where do they want to go, and c) what's keeping them from getting there?

Where are they now?
- What do they know and don't know about your proposal?
- What is their attitude towards what you're proposing?
- What concerns will they have?

Where do they want to go?
- What organizational goals do they support?
- How are they measured?
- What are the interests of their department or function?
- What are their personal goals and aspirations?

What's keeping them from getting there?
Needs arise in four ways. This one's pretty simple, if you just keep in mind the acronym POCR (pronounced "poker"):
- *Problems:* known problems or deficiencies they're struggling with.
- *Opportunities:* nothing is broken, but there is a better way to do things.

- *Changes:* things have changed in their world that they need to respond to.
- *Risks:* potential problems that could arise.

These are just a few of the questions you should consider and actively work to answer. While it takes you more time and effort up front, it can save you a lot of time in the long run. The questions will have to be answered at some point, so why wait until they are asked, and then have to schedule another conversation— sometimes more than once?

These questions will help you increase the value you provide by tailoring your message and your approach to the unique needs of your listeners. The closer you can come to expressing the *why* in terms that are unique to them, the more value you will add. For example, you could recommend an idea because it will "save money", and you will sound just like everyone else they've heard that day. Or, you could say, "The money it will save will free up X dollars to focus on your favorite Project Y." A statement like that does two things for you. Like throwing darts, the sharper the point, the greater the chance it will stick. Second, it sends a clear message that you have invested time in seeing things from their point of view, which certainly can't hurt your credibility or the relationship.

Intrinsic needs

As we've already seen in the discussion about WIFU, man does not "live by bread alone", so the people on the other end of your communication also have needs and wants besides objective and rational self-interest. Even in business decisions, the *why* can often be deeply personal or emotional, and no less important for not being measurable.

You've heard the trite old saying: "Give a man a fish and you feed him for a day; teach him to fish and you feed him for life." It applies to communication and persuasion as well. Extrinsic incentives used to get behavior change are like giving them a fish. It's quick and also doesn't take much thought, but often the desired behavior only lasts as long as you have the ability to a) monitor the behavior and b) furnish the necessary reward or punishment. If you want to drive lasting behavior change, you've got to find ways to get people to do things for their own reasons, and the best way to do this is to use their sense of who they are—the type of person they consider themselves to be, or aspire to be—to provide internal, long-lasting motivation.

Simply put, people have a deeply embedded sense of who they are, and how they should act in specific situations as a result. Sociologist James March said that when confronted with a decision, people make a rapid unconscious calculation that answers these questions: What kind of situation is this? Who am I? What does a person such as I do in this type of situation?[10] Our identities—who we are and how we see ourselves—are extremely important to us.

Each of us is made up of different layers of identities: professional, organizational, religious, national, social and family, and various situations may evoke the decision rules for one of our particular facets as called for. That's why it's not surprising that firefighters were insulted by the offer of a popcorn popper to consider a safety video.

Because they are more personal and private, there are two problems with using intrinsic appeals. First, they may be harder to discover, although you can find clues in understanding the corporate norms and values. Second, intrinsic reasons can also be difficult to talk about directly, as they may be seen as too personal, so you must use tact in addressing them.

Yet given all that, they are still powerful motivators, and many times trump objective personal interests. For example, most people have a strongly developed sense of fairness and will often reject offers that will leave them better off just to punish someone they think is acting unfairly.

There is much more to intrinsic motivators than can be covered in this book, but one key need is so important that it's built into the criteria for determining value: relationship needs.

Relationship needs

Respect for people is a core element in lean thinking, and it should be obvious why relationships are such an important part of the value equation. Maintaining amicable relationships and respect for individuals is the right thing to do, full stop. But it's also good business and communication practice, because it makes it much more likely that others will listen to you, trust what you say, and act upon what you tell them when they feel valued and respected. And, unless you're a complete misanthrope, it's simply much more pleasant to work in such an environment.

One of the best ways to respect the relationship is to get into the habit of bringing a gift to every communication opportunity. Give people a gift, and they feel compelled to respond in kind. How does this apply to a conversation? You certainly don't walk in hand them a physical gift; at the very least it's awkward and insincere, and it could even be illegal.

But you can give them the social gifts of attention, respect, and validation. If you treat people right, they will respond the same way. Instead of focusing on whether you impress the other person, try to show you're impressed with them. Instead of trying to look competent, try to make them feel competent. Instead of talking about yourself, get them to talk about themselves. If you want people to like you, like them first. If you want people to trust you, trust them first. If you want people to open up about themselves, open up about yourself. In other words, you go first and meet them more than halfway.

Build Your Outside-In Thinking Muscle

So, how do you boost your outside-in thinking? It's not so much a skill you need to learn; it's an ability you already have that you need to be reminded to use. It's like listening: we all have the ability to do it well—when we remember to do it and make the effort, kind of like having a useful feature on your smartphone that you forget to use. Ironically, the best way to get what you want is to stop thinking about what you want and start thinking about what the other person wants. It's wise to heed the words of Charlie Greene: "Don't think less of yourself, but think about yourself less".[11]

It's important to note that cognitive empathy takes place in the brain's executive function areas, unlike emotional empathy, which is activated in the limbic system. What this means in plain English is that it does take work, but you can activate it by paying attention—reminding yourself to think about it and willing yourself to pay attention to the other side's perspective.

We've seen already that we don't automatically apply outside-in thinking. First, because we're naturally egotistical, so we tend to approach things from our own perspective. And, because our own perspective already exists in our minds, and someone else's perspective has to be actively brought out, it takes work. It requires what Daniel Kahneman calls System 2 thinking, and our brains resist making any more effort than necessary.

Fortunately, research has shown that simply reminding yourself to take the other person's perspective will make you much better at it. Reminding yourself "activates" the script in your brain. For example, when people participate in a group task, and then are asked how important their own contribution was to the final result, they usually grossly overestimate their share. But, if the same people are asked to first consider what others contributed, and then asked the question, the estimates of their own contribution drop considerably.[12]

It's pretty obvious that if you take the time to prepare for an important meeting, especially using the questions listed in the previous section, you can't help but activate your outside-in thinking ability. But outside-in thinking is useful in all conversations, including questioner-led or chance encounters, and in these cases you need to prime it by reminding yourself to answer <u>the question</u>.

The longer term benefit is that if you remind yourself to activate your outside-in thinking ability enough times, eventually it can become a habit, and it will make you a much more valuable communicator.

The Limits Of Outside-In Thinking

It's crucially important to realize that outside-in thinking has limits. Regardless of how much you learn about what drives the other person, you are almost certain to get at least part of it wrong. No matter how close you are to a person, it's impossible to consistently predict how they will react to your message.

That's the bad news. The good news is that you can adjust when you realize you haven't hit the target exactly, through effective dialogue, which is covered in its own section to come.

2

Lean Communication Key #2: Have a Clear Purpose

Call to Action
Have a clear purpose and intent for every communication.

Summary
This chapter addresses the <u>what</u> side of <u>the question</u>. You must be clear in your own mind about what your intent is for the communication, and also make it explicit to the listener early in the conversation. When the ask is clear, it helps both parties to organize their thinking and figure out how to respond.

Answering the *What* side of <u>the Question</u>

> *"I want to talk about me*
> *Want to talk about I*
> *Want to talk about number one*
> *Oh my me my*
> *What I think, what I like, what I know, what I want, what I see"*
> Toby Keith

You will recall that communication value derives not only from improving outcomes but from answering <u>the question</u> in the listener's mind:

What do you want me to do and *why* should I do it?

We began with the *why* side of the question, because value is ultimately determined by the end customer, or listener. But, just as a manufacturer aims to earn a profit from selling its products, you're perfectly justified in striving to maximize your own returns from communicating. Essentially, you work and communicate to further your own goals and support your own interests, and of course there's nothing wrong with that. Lean communication is not a prescription for rolling over and being a doormat and sacrificing your interests for everyone else.

Lean communication is a tool to help you, so the *what* half of the question is also critically important. You communicate to improve outcomes, and your own personal outcomes should certainly rank up there in importance with those of others. And the really nice part about it is that focusing on the *what* question actually adds value to the other party as well.

Having a clear purpose benefits every aspect of the RoTE equation. It can improve the return for each party, reduce the effort and time to make a decision, and improve the relationship.

Answering the what question helps the other party
Although the ask may seem to be all about you, it actually helps the other party as well. That's because it takes the onus off them to do the hard work of sifting through a mass of material and makes it easier for them to decide.

Do the heavy lifting for them
One of the best ways to add maximum value to the other person is to do most of the work for them. Do you deliver a finished product, or is some assembly required?

According to an apocryphal story, when Henry Kissinger became President Nixon's National Security Adviser in 1969, he brought a reputation as a demanding taskmaster. So, when a staffer was given an assignment to write a position paper for his new boss, he understandably put in extra hours and took great pains to produce top-notch work. A day after he had turned it in, Kissinger called him into his office and asked him, "Is this the best you can do?"

The staffer gulped, promised he could improve it, and went back to his desk. He cancelled his other appointments, called his wife to tell her he would be home very late, and worked feverishly on the report: fine-tuning it, adding information, clarifying where necessary, etc. At the end of the week, he turned it in. On Monday morning, Kissinger passed by and contemptuously dropped the report on his desk. In a loud voice, he again asked, "Is *this* the best you can do?"

Stunned and not a little frustrated, the staffer vowed to do even better, and redoubled his efforts from the previous week, putting even longer hours and finding even better ways to express and support his position. Two days later, convinced that it was as close to perfect as he could get it, he turned it in again. The next day, Kissinger again asked, "Is this *really* the best you can do?"

The aide had finally had enough, so he looked at Kissinger squarely and said, "Yes, that is the best I can do."

Kissinger replied, "Good. *Now* I will read it."

Kissinger could have read the first draft himself and—with a little thinking—had what he needed to make a decision, but he got more value from having his staffer do that work for him. He made the staffer do the work so he would not have to—not because he was lazy, but because he had so many other important things to do with his time. In economics, it's called comparative advantage—even if you can do something better than someone else, you're better off paying another person to do it and using your time for higher value activities.

Suppose you go to your executive team to propose a project. You want them to make an informed decision, so you give them a data dump of every fact that is in your head. This way, you ensure that they will know as much as you do about it, so they can apply their superior vision and judgment to can make a better decision than you could by yourself.

Don't follow the old Fox News slogan: "We report, you decide." It is a nice sentiment for a reporter, but that's not what you are. You need to do more than report—you need to at least advocate for a position. If you present all the information that's in your head without analysis or recommendation, you are asking the other person to do your work for you.

What value have you added in that case? At least you have collected the relevant data, so that's a good thing. But they still have to do a lot of the work of interpreting the data, sifting out the critical from the irrelevant, making judgments about the accuracy and truth, and so on.

Thinking is hard work, and it takes time. Especially if you're communicating upwards, your listeners are perfectly capable of handling the hard work of thinking, but rarely do they have the time to put the required depth of thought into every decision they have to make every day. It's like buying furniture from Ikea: you save money but then you have to assemble it yourself.

Anything you can do to ease this "cognitive strain" on your listener, will make your message more persuasive and actually more pleasurable to listen to.[1]

In another context, Samuel Johnson said: "What is written without effort is read without pleasure." If you want to maximize your chances of getting through to the other person, keeping their attention, and getting the agreement that will benefit both parties, *you* have to do the work.

Make it easier to decide and act
Besides saving your listeners the hard work of thinking, you can

also add value by making it easier for them to decide. While you can't make the decision for them, you can recommend a decision after you've done all the initial hard work of eliminating all other possibilities. By doing this work for them, you add more value by making it easier and faster for them to decide.

It may be counterintuitive, but you add value by limiting their choices. Their perception of the value they receive from communicating with you depends to a certain extent on the perceived effort to decide. While it seems like common sense that giving the other person a greater degree of freedom would be more valuable to them, that's not so.

There is some convincing research that demonstrates that when it comes to choice, more is actually less. For example, Columbia professor Sheena Iyengar has found that participation in 401-K plans fell as the number of choices proliferated, *and* decision quality in general deteriorated. In another well-known experiment, she compared what happened when a booth was set up in a store featuring choices of fruit jams. When consumers faced a choice with 24 flavors, 60% of people stopped at the booth, compared to only 40% when there were only six flavors. But only 3% of tasters actually bought a jar when there were more choices, compared to 30% who chose among a smaller selection.[2]

Why does this happen? It's probably because decision-making is actually hard work that requires willpower, and making too many decisions can deplete the decider's willpower reserves. Psychologist Roy Baumeister has found that it's not just the mental effort of taking in and analyzing information that's taxing, but that the act of actually making a decision depletes reserves of willpower even more.[3]

Think about your "customer" for a minute: the person whom you're asking to make a decision based on the information you provide. A top executive is essentially an engine for making decisions, and they have to make a lot of them. That does not mean it gets easier for them. They still suffer from decision fatigue just like anyone else, so you do them a favor by simplifying the decision for them.

Answering the what question helps you

Clearly answering the *what* question helps you in three ways. It makes it more likely you will get what you want, it makes you more credible, and it helps you clarify your own thinking.

It boosts the chances of getting what you want

Knowing what you want increases the chances you will get it. If you're explaining a situation to someone, it may be the first time they've thought about it, so they simply can't put the same time into thinking about it that you have. There is a good chance that they will be at least slightly uncertain about what to do—your recommended decision acts as an anchor for their final decision, and anchors can set the terms of the discussion.

Do not be reluctant to ask for what you want. As negotiation expert G. Richard Shell writes, "Research shows that people with specific, high aspirations tend to accomplish more than people who have vague, do-my-best goals."[4]

If you think of any communication as a transaction in which both parties negotiate for optimum value, it's clear that transactions add the most value when both parties emerge better off. The side that enters a negotiation with the clearest prior idea of their goals and limits tends to get more of what they seek. It's like attacking from a fortified position. So, knowing what "price" to ask—what you want—will increase your own return on time and effort.

It conveys confidence and credibility

Being clear about what you want also makes you look more credible and puts you on a more equal footing with the other person. It raises you from someone supplying inputs for a decision to an active participant in the value creation process. Decision makers generally don't like people who bring problems to them without at least suggesting a solution. They don't have to agree with the proposed solution, but they will appreciate the fact that you've thought about it.

There's an old saying that you can get a lot done if you don't care who gets the credit, but you gain clout in an organization by getting others to do what you advocate—and by being seen as the originator of the ideas. You can't get credit for actions that you didn't suggest.

It clarifies your own thinking

Being clear about your ask entails some personal risk, as it shines a light on your personal judgment. That should force you to think more deeply and clearly as you figure out what to recommend. So, for example, if you're recommending a solution to a problem you've identified, you are much more likely to critically analyze the root causes, think broadly about alternatives, and look ahead to potential consequences. That level of thinking should improve the quality of the end product, which is the best ultimate driver of your personal credibility.

Answering the **what** question saves time for both parties

Answering the *what* question saves a lot of time, both for your listener and for you. It saves time for them, because when they know what you want, they can more easily organize and make sense of the incoming information, and they will let you know what they need to give you agreement.

You do run the risk of getting a quick rejection, but if you were going to end up with a no anyway, it's better to lose early than late. Besides saving time, it may avoid a protracted debate that makes the other person stick even more to their own position.

Answering the *what* question also saves you time, for two reasons. First, it forces you to think hard about what the other person values and needs, which makes for quicker and more enduring agreements. Second, as you will see in upcoming chapters, it helps you to find the right words and to strip away anything that does not directly contribute to answering <u>the question</u>.

Answering the what *question improves the relationship*

Besides reducing waste by saving time, being clear up front about your ask respects the relationship by reducing tension. Think of the times that someone has approached you for a request—you know they want something but they don't get right to the point, so you feel more and more uncomfortable as they beat around the bush, because you're wondering where they're going with it. By letting the person know up front what your *ask* is, it makes for a much smoother and pleasant discussion. As Alan Palmer says in his book, *Talk Lean*, "…every minute which passes at the beginning of a meeting before you announce your real intentions will generate either suspicion or caution."[5] In most cases, others will appreciate your direct and transparent approach.

What should you ask for?

In some ways, because you know your own thinking so well, it would seem that the *what* is easy; it's certainly easier than trying to get into the listener's head and figure out what would best motivate them.

You're going to ask for whatever serves your purposes, so of course your *ask* can be whatever you want it to be. But even lean communication is not going to be a magic solution that will get you everything you want every time. You need to be realistic, especially since asking and being rejected can make your task harder. If someone is opposed to your idea, and you don't change their minds, you run the risk of strengthening, rather than weakening, their initial beliefs.[6] So, take care to distinguish between your own wants and needs. In other words, be strategic about what you ask for.

That's why the *what* depends a lot on where you are in the decision process. If the listener is opposed to your idea, it's probably not realistic to swing for the fences and win them over to enthusiastic support in one conversation or presentation. You'll need to nudge the needle in the direction you want, because pushing too hard risks making them dig in their heels and possibly shutting the door entirely to your *ask*. Instead of going for final approval, you could ask them to keep an open mind and schedule another meeting, or give the go-ahead to form an exploratory task force to further develop the idea.

If they are neutral on your idea, what you ask for depends on why they're neutral. If they're unaware of the situation, you need to educate them, so they can decide whether it's something that merits their attention. If they know about it but don't see why they should care, you need to bring out the costs and consequences and get them to agree that the situation needs to be addressed. If they want do so something but haven't decided what to do about it, your *ask* will be the solution you recommend.

If they're already positive about your idea, your *ask* is likely going to be action-oriented: you may need to move them to take action, which may be to take the next step, or to sell your idea to the decision makers.

How to ask
Presumably your listeners will weigh your ask on its merits, but as in so often in communication, how you say it can carry a lot of weight as well. Here are a few ways to boost your chances of compliance.

Don't be afraid to ask
No one likes rejection, so we often hold back on asking for something because we are afraid of being told no. In fact, according to a series of studies conducted by psychologists Francis Flynn and Vanessa Lake,

we tend to overestimate the chance of rejection by about 100%. That's because we focus on the cost to the other party of saying yes, and don't focus enough on the cost to them of saying no.[7]

Adjust your attitude

The research just cited applied to situations where the requester is asking for a personal favor, but that's usually not you. If you've done the work to answer the *why*, you're actually doing them a favor by suggesting they do what you want. You're not a supplicant asking for their charity; you're making them an offer they should not refuse.

Be direct

Most communication situations benefit from being direct in your ask, so that there is no question in the other's mind what you expect from them. Do it early to reduce tension for both parties, and it will also help your cause by making you appear more confident.

Directness shows preparation, that you've carefully thought through the issue and you believe in the merits of what you're proposing.

Make it a statement not a question

Be direct in telling them what your ask is going to be, but don't frame it as an actual question: "Will you…?" That's because they don't have enough information yet, so their default answer is likely to be "No".

Instead, say something like: "My ask is going to be…" or "Once I've presented the options, I'm going to recommend that…"

If it's a formal meeting or presentation, you can list the ask as the last agenda item; when it's obvious to all concerned that the decision will be expected, it can do wonders to focus minds on a common purpose.

BE PREPARED TO ADJUST YOUR PURPOSE

Just as I closed the previous chapter on the limits of outside-in thinking, it's important to stress that you may need to be prepared to adjust your purpose as a result of the dialogue you have with your listener(s). You don't have a monopoly on all the good ideas, and you are probably missing some of the pieces of the puzzle that others might have. So, a willingness to listen and adapt may make a good idea even better. It will also help with the relationship. The tools to ensure that adaptability are covered in the Dialogue section.

If you get into the habit of putting value first every time you communicate, you could stop right here in this book and you would already become a much leaner communicator than most of your listeners will encounter. Even so, there still remain many opportunities to strip out waste and reduce their time and effort to realize that value, which is what we turn to next.

B

Brevity

Lean communication strives for maximum value with minimum waste, so it's time to turn our attention to the second part of that equation. While you must strive first of all to be an *effective* communicator, you also have to do it *efficiently* and that's what we cover in the next two chapters.

The next two chapters capture the essence of the word "lean": cutting out anything that does not add value to the ultimate customer. Lean communication is brief, concise, and succinct—and it's not repetitive to use all three words. In fact, brevity is technically the wrong word to use in this chapter: brief communication is merely short. Concise or succinct communication is short but packs a lot of meaning, or more bang for the buck.[1]

That said, we'll stick with brevity in this chapter because it keeps us focused on the time factor in the RoTE equation. Similar to a manufacturer of products, you want to create value for your customer but you also pay attention to how much you can charge in the marketplace. In the crowded attention marketplace, time is scarce and people begrudge every unnecessary minute they devote to your message.

Put yourself into the listener's place for a minute. Everybody wants value, but they want it at a reasonable price. Although your first consideration when you want to buy a product is the benefit you will receive from it, very close behind that is the question of whether you can afford it, or if it's worthwhile to pay the price even if you can. In addition, you would prefer to get only what you need when you need it, and not have to pay for what you won't use. If you've ever gone to a store like Costco and bought a humongous jar of something because it was great value, but only used a small amount of it, you already know this feeling.

Communication technology has made it so easy to churn out content that we are awash in immense floods of information. We get far more than we can ever use, and the vast majority of it goes to waste. In a perfect world, every single word would have its place and communication would have zero waste. It's almost impossible to achieve zero waste in most communication—indeed, it would be wasteful to strive too hard. We're not looking for perfection or poetry.

But there is still tremendous scope for improvement. It's easy to spot waste when you look for it. Have you ever asked someone a simple yes/no question and received a rambling dissertation in return? What about sitting through an interminable meeting just to get the few nuggets of information you need to do your job? Or maybe you were stuck listening to someone tell you all about their pet project even though it had no impact at all on your life. Here are just a few more examples of waste to reinforce the point:

- More information than needed
- Information that weakens the main message
- Vague wording that can be misunderstood or easily forgotten
- Words that spark unhelpful emotions
- Having unnecessary people in a meeting
- Rescheduling a meeting because you didn't have the right people
- Incorrect information
- Information they already know

The list could go on and on, but of course that would be wasteful.

How much time could you save if people communicating with you strove to eliminate anything that did not add value to you?

Brevity is not just efficient, it's also effective

While brevity brings obvious time-savings, it also can contribute to effective communication in three other ways: it improves understanding, it respects the relationship, and it adds to your personal credibility. Let's examine each in more detail:

Brevity improves understanding

More is often less when it comes to verbiage. Wordiness can interfere with understanding in three ways.

First, it can prevent the intended message from even getting through to the recipient, because you risk losing their attention. In this age of information overload, you are just one of many competitors for mindshare of everyone you speak to, particularly as you speak to higher levels within the organization. Just to be heard can be an accomplishment, and sustaining attention over time even more so. That places a premium on the ability to get your message across as quickly and efficiently as possible, because the listener's attention can be interrupted at any moment.

Second, wordiness can make it harder to grasp your message. Too much unnecessary information is like the pile of manure that hides the pony—it can obscure or dilute the main point of your message, so that they either miss it entirely or forget it when they need to apply the information. And even if your listeners are paying complete attention and making the effort to follow what you're saying, their working memory limits how much information they can absorb at one time, especially when an undue proportion of it is unrelated to the main point. It takes time to make sense of what you're saying and connect it to what they already know, and if they fall behind because you're pumping it out faster than they can absorb it, it's almost impossible to catch up.

Third, excessive talk can also make it difficult to get into the proper depth of discussion needed for a smart decision. If a meeting spends too much time in the early stages discussing irrelevant material, it may lead to hurried discussions in the remaining time, or to postponing to another meeting, which consumes yet more time.

Brevity respects the relationship

Brevity also respects the relationship, because it shows you care about their time. If you have ever avoided someone because you know they will take up too much of your time, or have been impatient for someone to get to the point, you know why you certainly don't want to be "that guy", the one who causes people to duck into the nearest office when they see him walking down the hall. At the very least, lack of brevity may cause people to tap other sources for information and take you out of the loop.

Business writing expert Josh Bernoff calls this idea The Iron Imperative: "Treat the reader's time as more valuable than your own."[2]

Personally, I love it when someone says, "I only have five minutes, so make it brief". I will accept the challenge and deliver my message with time to spare. When you do it right, it's funny how often they will give you even more time than they initially offered.

Brevity makes you more credible

There are some people who believe that more context and detail will make them seem more knowledgeable, but often the opposite is true. Fewer words—as long as they are delivering value--convey polish and confidence.

The effort to be brief disciplines your thinking; it forces you to think clearly about precisely what you want to say. That not only improves your message but adds to your own confidence in delivery, which makes you more credible.

Brevity in History

We like to think that our fast-paced world poses unique challenges to presenters because of the audience's impatience, but actually the need for brevity has been respected for thousands of years. Maybe the earliest story about brevity in public speaking was told by Herodotus, roughly 2,500 years ago.

If you think senior level audiences can be tough, imagine being an official from the city of Samia having to ask the Spartan authorities for aid after being driven from their city by the Persians. The Spartans, besides being fearsome warriors, were also renowned for their love of brevity.

When the delegation first spoke, they spoke so long that the Spartans said they had forgotten what they said at the beginning and didn't understand the rest.

The Samians tried again the next day, this time bringing an empty sack and simply saying: "This sack needs barley meal." The Spartans applauded their brevity and approved the request, although they did say the word "sack" could have been left out.

Two tools for brevity

The two principal lean communication elements to improve brevity are top-down explanation and the SO WHAT filter, which are covered in the next two chapters.

3

Lean Communication Key #3: Top-Down Communication

Call to action
Use a top-down structure to your communication—get your point out immediately and then support it as necessary.

Summary
The best way to be brief is to put your bottom line up front. Many people find this hard to do because they try to explain the situation or issue the same way they learned it, from the bottom up. Lean communication looks like an inverted pyramid, with the headline up front, the reasoning just below that, and supporting detail last.

Begin with your conclusion; it's the surest way to make your communication concise. The dictionary defines a conclusion as the result of your thinking—a deduction or inference. It may take you a long time and a lot of work—researching, learning and reasoning—to reach a conclusion, but that's no reason to put your listener through the same time and trouble that you endured.

Top-down communication is closely related to Answer <u>the</u> <u>Question</u>, but goes further. It also relates to how you unfold your reasoning and supporting detail after you've made your initial statement.

Top reasons for top-down communication

If there's a magic bullet in all of Lean Communication, it would have to be top-down communication, also known as BLUF: Bottom Line Up Front. That's because top-down explanations pay off beyond simply facilitating brevity; they also ensure value gets through, improve the relationship, promote clarity, and make you more persuasive and effective overall.

Above all, top-down supports value by maximizing the chances that your message will get through. As we've seen already, there's an epidemic of distraction in our society today, so it's critical to ensure that you take advantage of the fleeting window of opportunity you might have by front-loading your message.

We've already seen how getting your ask out early builds trust and reduces tension. Top-down carries the additional benefit of showing respect for the other person's time, which they will appreciate.

Top-down explanation also reduces waste via time savings, because when they know what the purpose of the conversation is, listeners will listen until they have heard enough to make a decision, or they will tell you exactly what they need to hear to give you what you want. By having shared agreement on the end product, you can both use dialogue to work and think *together* to produce the desired outcome. Sometimes they will give you what you want right away, which is always a good thing. They may, however, shut you down right away. That may not sound like a good thing, but if you're going to lose, it's better to lose early.

Top-down communication also contributes to clarity because it serves as an *advance organizer*: context that makes it easier for the listener to make sense of incoming information. Knowing the point of the incoming information makes it easier to organize in their mind, which makes it clearer to them.

For an illustration of how an advance organizer can help, read this paragraph and see if it makes sense to you:

"First you sort the items into like categories. Using color for sorting is common, but you can also use other characteristics, such as texture

or type of handling needed. Once you have sorted the items, you are ready to use the equipment. You want to process each category from the sorting separately. Place one category in the machine at a time."

How was that? Was it clear as mud to you? What if you had read this header before reading the paragraph: "Instructions for your new washing machine"?

In one experiment, students shown the context before they read the passage understood it almost 3X as well as those with no context.[1]

That's because, as John Medina, author of *Brain Rules*, says:

"The brain processes meaning before detail. Providing the gist, the core concept, first was like giving a thirsty person a tall glass of water. And the brain likes hierarchy. Starting with general concepts naturally leads to explaining information in a hierarchical fashion. You have to do the general idea first. And then you will see that 40 percent improvement in understanding."[2]

Finally, top-down is also more persuasive, for two reasons. First, it's direct, and direct is confident. How confident do you think you sound when you beat around the bush and appear afraid to come to the point? Second, it can put you in control of the conclusions. Our minds are pattern-generating machines: we try to make sense of incoming information by figuring out its meaning. If you give them all the detail before your conclusion, there is no guarantee that they will arrive at the same conclusion you have. They might reach a different conclusion, in which case you're further away than when you started.

Why we take too long to get to the point

If top-down explanation is so beneficial, what keeps us from doing it all the time? Why don't we get to the point immediately?

There are at least three reasons: lack of preparation, lack of confidence, and the mismatch between exploring and explaining.

When we don't prepare, it's easy to become long-winded because we think out loud, and usually the first time you say something it's not as clean and concise as it could be. It emerges from the mouth in half-baked form that forces us to backtrack, amend or edit what we just said.

Lack of preparation usually makes us less confident, which makes it harder to state directly what's on our minds; so we take tentative steps toward our conclusion, ready to retreat at the slightest sign of hesitation or displeasure on our counterpart's face. Another form of lack of confidence is that we try to impress the listener with how smart we are. I actually had someone in one of my classes admit that if he told his boss the answer straight away, his boss would not know how difficult it had been for him to figure it out!

Preparation and confidence are obvious, but there's a third reason that is much more subtle and takes a bit of explaining: the differences between learning something and explaining it to others.

How you learned it is not how you should explain it
We learn most of what we know from the bottom-up, because life does not present neat, logically-supported conclusions to us. In other words, we begin with detail and work to make sense of it.

For example, think about all the mental steps it takes to recommend a solution to a problem:

You may notice some details in a situation that suggest there's a problem, so you dig deeper. You collect data to figure out if the problem really exists, and you try to define exactly what the issue is. Next, you might think about whether its potential consequences make it a priority to be solved now. Assuming you proceed, you might try to figure out root causes, think of alternative solutions, and finally arrive at a decision or recommendation. That conclusion may take you a long time and the accumulation and analysis of a lot of detail to achieve.

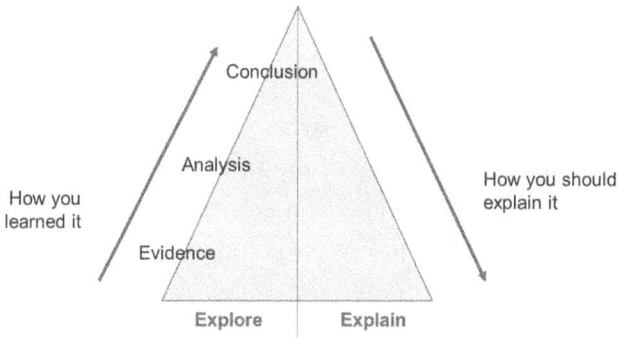

In general, we reach our conclusions in an upward process as shown on the left side above: we gather evidence, analyze it, and reach a conclusion. It can be a long, slow process to arrive at our point, with detours and false leads along the way.

As you can see, it can take a lot of time and effort to reach important conclusions for an effective decision or action, but once you have the answer, there is no reason to impose those costs on your listeners. Just because you made the long slow climb does not mean your listeners should have to.

That's why you add the most value by *starting* at the top, and then proceeding downhill to explain or support your point as necessary. The most efficient way to organize explanations, conversations, and presentations is top-down. Top-down communication adds value to the listener because if forces you to do the work for them—to make sense of the data and information and apply it to the necessary decision at hand. It forces you to present your finished thinking, or at least as close as you can get to it.

It doesn't always happen that way, of course. Sometimes we see a situation and get a sudden flash of insight—we vault to the top effortlessly because of our long experience. We use pattern recognition to avoid the hard slog of gathering and analyzing evidence. And that's perfectly acceptable as long as we don't need anyone else to concur with our conclusion. But the moment we need sign-off from someone else, we have to give them reasons, even if we think of those reasons after we've reached our conclusion.

Where have you seen this before? Top-down explanation is what you see in the typical newspaper story. The headline encapsulates the main point, the first paragraph contains the entire story in a nutshell, and then the rest of the story develops the detail.[3]

Scan the day's paper and you can easily see the value of top-down organization. In just a few seconds scanning the front page you can grasp the essentials of what's going on, because the headlines distill the essential news to just a few words. If you want to know a little more about a particular item, you can read the first paragraph. When you want to go in depth, you can then read the entire article if you choose. But the key is that, as the consumer of the information, *you* control how much information you receive.

Top-down structure revealed
Here's what top-down looks like:

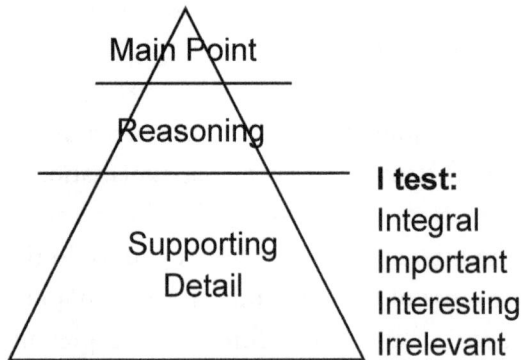

Ideally, this structure applies in almost any communication context, from delivering a formal presentation, initiating a conversation, answering a question, or even writing an email. Put your headline on top just as a newspaper does.

As Bill Lane, who was Jack Welch's speechwriter at GE for two decades, put it: "State clearly what you want right away. Give very little background. Offer very little methodology. Be clear about what it is *you want them to know.*"[4]

Begin with your main point, which is the answer to <u>the question</u>, followed by an outline of your reasoning to support it. You can then provide as much or as little supporting detail as they need to take the necessary decision or action.

Think of it as giving them the "minimum viable product", or MVP. In business, an MVP is a way of getting to market quickly with a product that works, that just does what it's supposed to do, rather than delaying launch to pack in features to try to please everyone. In effect, an MVP is a best-guess hypothesis about what the listener needs. It's not a stab in the dark, because it's based on your knowledge of the "customer" and your analysis of the situation.

It might be useful to think about your message in terms of the 80/20 Rule. Probably 80% of the value of what you're saying is contained in 20% of your words, so if you can choose the right information to lead with, you can deliver 80% of value in 20% of the time. That leaves 80% of the available time to have a productive dialogue and create additional value.

Or look at it another way. Assume that you will be cut off by your listeners only 20% of the way into your allotted time. Would you have given them most of what they need to make a decision? If not, you might want to go back and work harder on front-loading your message.

As you can see from the diagram, there are four levels of supporting detail in descending order of relevance to your message, and we'll cover those in greater detail in the next chapter. For now, consider the supporting detail as "background", and remember that they call it background because that's where it belongs.

It's important to note that top-down does not mean superficial; depth of knowledge is still important, but you should not lead with it. Often you have to be prepared for a deep dive: there may be a thread in the conversation that a specialist would want to follow, or a senior executive who is not a specialist might scratch the surface to test the depth of your knowledge. In fact, having a facile and fluent command of facts and detail has a strong subliminal effect in its own right. We are impressed by those who have a deep grasp of their topic, who can pull up concrete and specific facts to support their arguments.

Deep knowledge can also make your communication more compelling by adding specificity and concrete detail. It's one thing to say that your product makes your customer's business process more efficient; it's far better to say, "We speed up the reconcilement process by 35%, which cuts an average of four days out of your accounts receivable."

Top-down communication in practice

Top-down communication can apply in almost any communication situation or medium. Here are four of the most common.

Presentations

As we've seen, when an audience at a presentation gets the context up front, they find it easier to understand and process the incoming information, and they are better able to ask relevant questions about your proposal. So, you need to be clear at the beginning what you are asking for and why it's important. For example, you might begin by saying,

"I'm here to get your approval for two additional software engineers for my team, to respond to changes in the scope of the project since we last met. I'll start with a high-level overview of what's changed, what it means for the department, and how we plan to address the key issues that have come up, and then go into each section is as much depth as necessary."

When you say this, you could have your agenda slide showing on the screen to help orient the audience to where you are. On the other hand, you might consider keeping the screen blank, so that you can simply talk to the audience, gauge their response, and then get their agreement to proceed.

Meetings or one-on-one conversations

If the setting is a little less formal than a presentation, such as dropping by someone's office for chat, how does it differ? Actually, not much. There should not be a substantial difference between the two—they're both still conversations. The only change is that you probably won't have slides showing on a screen behind you. If you initiate the conversation or the request, recall that the question is "What do you want me to do and why?" So, for example, you can begin by saying:

"I need a one-time budget variance to take advantage of a unique opportunity…"

Having said that, you may not need to go any further. Pay attention to their response and add detail if you think it's necessary or if they ask for more. You can go as deep into the supporting detail as they ask for. You might have to cover everything, but maybe they will home in on your first reason, and ask you to prove it. Once you do that, they may be satisfied.

Email

Email is probably the best reason to use top-down communication, not only because we're inundated in it, but also because the recipient can so easily ignore or dismiss the message because they don't have to be polite and at least pretend to pay attention. Most people need a very good reason to read beyond the first paragraph, so everything of importance should be contained in it. A useful rule of thumb is to try to limit your message to what fits in the preview screen of the typical smartphone. In fact, go one step further and distill that paragraph into a headline and put that in the subject line. (If there were a way to switch the word "headline" with "subject" in your email program, it would probably have a huge impact on our GDP.)

Answering questions

Top-down works especially well when you're answering a direct question, although it's best described as "answer first". Most times, it's not an esoteric skill; it's something you already know how to do as a functioning human being—you simply listen carefully to the question and try to give them what they need as succinctly as possible. Even if the answer requires some background to make sense to them, try to give the short answer first and then drop down the pyramid as you need to.

Although it's not an esoteric skill, there are some useful techniques that can help you deliver crisp and confident answers, which we cover in Chapter 8.

Limits of Top-down communication

Let me quickly remind you once again that lean communication is simply a tool, and it does not apply in every situation. There are times where top-down communication may not work or might even be counterproductive.

When the audience is opposed to your idea to begin with, putting your *ask* up front may cause them to raise the drawbridge, and immediately shut down attention or begin forming counterarguments in their mind before you have a chance to give your reasoning. In this case you would be wiser to be more indirect in your approach. In the Dialogue section, we'll look at ways to use lean questions and lean listening to examine the situation and jointly craft an approach to realizing value.

Finally, answer-first may get you in trouble if the questioner is not asking in good faith—for example, trying to trap you into a simplistic answer as if they are a prosecutor in a courtroom. Once again, you have to use your own judgment when Lean Communication applies.

Top-down communication is an excellent and necessary start, but most times it is not enough. You will still have to defend your main point with reasoning and supporting detail. The trick is not to overdo it, and for that, we turn to lean communication key #4: the So What Filter.

4

Lean Communication Key #4:
So What Filter

Call to action
Apply the So What filter to ensure that you communicate only information that is <u>integral</u> to your point or otherwise <u>important</u> to your listeners.

Summary
Everyone hears and processes messages through the So What filter: what does it mean to me? You can eliminate a lot of wasteful communication by applying the filter before the words come out of your mouth. So what is your mental tool for ensuring that everything you say adds value and makes sense. You learn how to apply the 4-I test to your content to eliminate the irrelevant and use interesting information to strengthen your message.

> *"Writing is easy. All you have to do is cross out the wrong words."*
> Mark Twain

Twain's advice is spot-on, and also absolutely useless—unless you could apply a tool that would enable you to figure out which words to keep and which to cross out. This chapter provides a simple and powerful tool to do just that.

Here's the tool: One of the best ways to achieve lean communication mastery would be to write—better yet, tattoo—these two crucial words on the palm of your left hand: *SO WHAT?* Then whenever you're in a conversation with someone, use it as a filter for your thoughts: glance down at your hand every so often to remind yourself that everything you say should support, reinforce, or extend your main point. And, since your main point should be about improving outcomes for your listener, you will ensure that you are delivering information that they will find useful.

Obviously, you're not going to go around with *so what* scribbled on your palm, but you should work on using *so what* as the internal mental filter you slip into that micropause between thought and utterance, to sift out anything that does not contribute to your main point. The *so what* question forces you to consider your message from the point of view of the other person and weed out irrelevancies.

That may seem like a tall order, but your mind processes words about four times faster than you speak, so you have time to choose your words if you work at it. It's like you're editing your thoughts on the fly. After a while, it becomes a habit that avoids a tremendous amount of waste. Of course, if you have time to prepare before you speak or write, it's much easier and there is no excuse for not doing so.

So what is about two things, value and coherence. The first is the connection to value, to what the listener cares about. Typically, they will be listening through their own self-interest filter—WIFM or WIFU—because that's where the value is. It's their shorthand for asking:

- Why should I care?
- Why should I keep listening to you?
- What am I getting out of this conversation?
- Where's the value to me or to the larger picture?

- What do I do with this information?
- How can I use this?

The *so what* filter is your vehicle for taking personal responsibility to ensure that value is being delivered. Even more, asking *so what* is about making it impossible *not* to focus on value.

So what also tests for logical coherence, making sure that what you say directly follows from or supports your main point. In other words, does it help answer <u>the question</u>? Years ago, when I ran the credit department for a bank, I would read reports in which junior analysts would write about a prospective borrower's recent financial performance. Most of these were what we called "elevator reports", because they were full of phrases such as "sales went up 7%, while costs went down 2%..." It's easy to fill up several pages of descriptive information such as this, and still never answer <u>the question</u>, which in these cases was, "Should we make the loan?" I would return their reports with a big *so what* scribbled next to every paragraph that failed to connect the facts to <u>the question</u>.

Toyota made famous the practice of the 5 Whys; lean communication will get you to apply the 5 *So Whats*. When you're trying to figure out what something means to your listener, don't stop at your first answer. Keep asking *So What* until you reach a meaningful—and potentially valuable—impact or outcome. Our supply reliability is higher. *So what?* You will be assured of getting what you need. *So what?* You can place smaller order sizes. *So what?* You will have greater flexibility to adjust to changes in demand. *So what?* You can increase revenues by adapting to the market.

Here's another example:

My approach eliminates three of the seven steps.
So What?
You can get the testing done faster.
So What?
We'll complete the prototype ahead of time.

So What?
It will let us get the product to market first.
So What?
It will increase our market share.
So what?
You'll get a much-needed win.
OK, sounds good. Let's do it.

In real life, each of these examples would make for overly long and possibly awkward conversations if the listener had to keep asking so what until they were satisfied. By applying the *so what* filter in their thinking before the words emerge from the mouth, a lean communicator can cut right to the heart of the matter. In effect, you're answering the why question for them.

How explicit should you be in expressing the *so what*? It's a judgment call. If the *so what* is obvious, you run the risk of appearing patronizing and insulting the listener's intelligence. On the other hand, implications that you take for granted may not automatically occur to the other person, or vice versa. When you say you have ten years' experience, you may think it would reassure the other side, but they may conclude that it means your ideas are outdated. That's another reason it's important to know your audience. With mixed audiences, it's better to err on the side of explicitness.

Use *So What* to Apply the 4-I-Test

When you broach a topic with someone, you know far more about the situation you're discussing than you need to tell the listener, so it helps to have a way to figure out what's value and what's waste. Taiichi Ohno, one of the founding fathers of lean thinking, said that eliminating waste is not difficult—spotting waste is.

The Four-I test is a tool for spotting waste. I got the idea from something I read a long time ago in an old Boy Scout Handbook. The handbook suggested that you should empty out your backpack and make three piles after your first campout. The first pile would contain things you used every day; the second, things that you used occasionally; the third, things that you did not use at all. For the next campout, leave the latter two piles at home.

The Four-I test is similar, but a bit more forgiving. It consists of four "piles" of information that may find their way into your communication: integral, important, interesting, and irrelevant.

Integral

Integral information is absolutely essential to your main point; without it, your message does not make sense or your proposal is unsupported. At the very least, it's the *what* and the *why*, including the strongest reasons to do what you're asking. It may also include root cause analysis of the problem, evidence that something works, cause and effect relationships, key assumptions etc. Integral information is the 20% that provides 80% of the meaning of your message.

Important

Important information is additional material that can help others make sense of your message, address their particular concerns, or furnish strong additional support as necessary. Examples of important information might include: alternatives considered but rejected, research methods used, sample sizes, what the effect will be on the overtime budget, etc.

Another type of important information is evidence or reasons in favor of your proposal that are relevant but not necessarily your strongest. For example, you may be able to think of seven reasons to move forward, but it's better to choose your three strongest and keep the others in reserve in case you need it. This will prevent your important evidence from crowding out the integral evidence.

The distinction between integral and important is often a judgment call, and of course the ultimate judges are your listeners, because they are the ones who control agreement or non-agreement. You may think that the effect your proposal will have on the overtime budget at the warehouse is not integral to the decision, but someone in the audience may think it's critical.

Your best bet is to know your audience and make your best guess as to what they need to know, to act on the information you give them. Err on the side of leanness, but be prepared to answer anticipated questions, or contain the important information in your backup slides, in case you need it.

Interesting

Probably the most dangerous type of information you have, is what cognitive psychologist Richard Mayer calls seductive detail. There are two reasons for this. First, you are not always the best judge of what others will find interesting, especially if you're passionate about your topic. As Dennis Hopper said, "Just because it happened to you doesn't make it interesting." For example, when I ask my students how many of them like to talk about their children, most hands in the room go up; but when I ask them how many of them like to hear others talk about their children, almost all hands drop immediately.

And even if others do find it interesting, but it does not support your main point, it can stick in their attention and crowd out the integral and important detail. Mayer studied the effect that seductive detail has on science textbooks, many of which include little factoids and sidebars to keep it interesting for students. For example, in a passage about how lightning forms, they may cite some statistics about how many people are killed yearly by lightning. Mayer found that the inclusion of material that's meant to engage interest without being relevant to the main message results in significantly less learning.[1]

There's still a judgment call here. A key part to ensuring listeners receive value is that they remember the information they need when it comes time to make the decision. As we will see later in Chapter 7, interesting information in the form of stories, or vivid examples *that support the integral and important* can be useful to help your listeners retain what you told them.

It all comes back to *so what*. Simply put, if it's interesting and relevant, use it. Otherwise kill it.

Irrelevant

This is the mass of detail that's left over; if it does not add value to the listener or does not support your main point, it does not belong. While no one sets out to purposely include irrelevant material, it forces its way in for several reasons:

- *Self-serving excuses or boasting.* When you want to make yourself look good, you might talk about how hard you've been working or the difficulties you've overcome to get the information.
- *Information compulsion.* This phenomenon was described by journalist Tom Wolfe, who said, "People have an overwhelming need to tell you something that you don't know, even when it's not in their best interest."[2]
- *Excessive context.* Decisions are about the future, but too many people spend far too much time talking about how we got to this point rather than where we need to go next.
- *Editorial commentary.* It's tempting to tell people how they should react to a situation, but sometimes the facts best speak for themselves.
- *Neat stuff.* Have you ever come across a visual or a chart that is just so cool that you have to include it in your presentation? Before you do, ask yourself what point it serves or how it advances your argument.
- *Boilerplate.* You see a lot of this in presentations; it includes such things as opening amenities, your "corporate story", and all the stuff your legal and marketing departments force you to put on your slides.

The Four-I Test is not always as straightforward as it may seem, because it depends on who is in the audience and what you know about them. You may think it's integral to your argument to explain the consequences of the problem, but if they already know that, it may slip all the way to irrelevant information. You may think that the source for a certain chart would be slightly above irrelevant, but an audience member may have had a bad experience with information from that source in the past, and it could then turn into a crucial piece of information. Once again, remember Lean Key #1: Make it about them.[3]

A Warning against Applying the 4-I Test Too Severely

Beware of applying the 4-I test too severely. I've mentioned judgment several times already in this chapter, and it bears repeating. By being overzealous, you may harm the relationship or potentially lose the chance to create value. Let me explain each of these in turn.

Taken literally, common courtesies such as opening amenities in a presentation (thank you for letting me be here, etc.), or social softeners, flourishes (I think you'll agree that…) are "waste", because they don't add value to your main point. Yet we're not all purely analytical information processing machines, and social conventions can help preserve the relationship, just as saying something in a less direct way can make it more palatable (as we cover in greater detail in Chapter 6).

Repetition is also technically wasteful; if you've already said it, what value do you add by repeating it? Actually, ensuring value is precisely why repetition can be essential. The first imperative of lean communication is to ensure that value gets across, and it does not always stick the first time it's uttered. Your listeners may have not paid complete attention, or they may not have fully bought into your logic. So, if you said it and it did not have its full effect, what you said was wasted. Churchill said it best:

"If you have an important point to make, don't try to be subtle or clever. Use a pile driver. Hit the point once. Then come back and hit it again. Then hit it a third time – a tremendous whack."

But if you decide to repeat something, try to make it interesting by expressing it in a slightly different way.

How Long Should a Presentation Be?

Supposedly, Abraham Lincoln was asked how long a man's legs should be, and he replied: "Long enough to reach the ground." I'm reminded of this story whenever people ask me how long presentations should be, so I usually tell them, "long enough to make your point."

That's true, but—like Lincoln's answer—not completely helpful, so I suggest two additional rules:

1. Shorter than you think
2. Shorter than the time allotted

Shorter than you think. In my classes, I usually require participants to prepare a seven minute presentation. There's no special magic in that exact length; it's driven by time considerations in the class. Several years ago, I was explaining this requirement to a group of mid-level executives in Rome, and they told me that I was delusional, that what they had to say was much more complicated than could be squeezed into seven minutes. I asked them to humor me and try to do it anyway.

On the following day, their presentations went so well that the senior person in the room told me they would henceforth institute a seven-minute rule in Europe for their presentations.

Others are slightly more lenient, but not by much. Bill Lane, who was Jack Welch's speechwriter at GE for two decades, suggests ten minutes. "Ten minutes is more than enough time to present effectively on most subjects, if you think it through and extract every non-contributing thought or word."[4]

Interestingly, ten minutes is the time limit suggested by psychologist John Medina in his book, *Brain Rules.*[5] He tells us that audiences begin to check out at that point, so you have to shake things up or move to a different point to keep their attention.

At a normal speaking rate of 125 words per minute, the amount of information that you can pack into a ten-minute presentation is equal to about five double-spaced pages of writing. If you can't say what you need to say in that time, you're probably not thinking clearly enough about what your key point is, or you're trying to do too much. When you consider that Winston Churchill used to require every memo sent to him not to exceed one page no matter how big the topic, you can see how it's possible, especially since you're not fighting a world war.

Shorter than the time allotted. Parkinson's Law does not have to apply to presentations: your message does not have to expand to fill the time allotted to it. I know you might think that this is your one big chance in the limelight to be noticed, but taking too much time is one of the best ways to ensure that it *is* your only shot. If they give you 30 minutes, plan for 15-20 (if that). If they give you ten, plan for seven.

There are two reasons for this. First, if what you're saying has any interest at all to the audience, they will interrupt you with questions, especially those higher up in the organization. You *want* questions and dialogue, but if you have too much stuff prepared you're going to feel forced to get it all out. Second, what are the chances someone will complain if you take less time than was on the schedule? In fact, you may not have a choice, because chances are anyone on the agenda before you did not prepare as well as you did and has already eaten into your time. I've had plenty of speaking engagements or presentations where the organizer has asked me if I can shorten my talk because something changed on the schedule. I've *never* had someone tell me that something changed, and could I please talk for a bit longer than planned?

Incidentally, the other benefit of the inverted pyramid structure is that it affords you tremendous flexibility to compress or elongate your presentation as needed. That's because you can add or omit detail as needed to match your time constraints, without sacrificing the most important information.

Top-down Communication and the So What Filter both make your communication efficient by reducing your listeners' time investment. Next we turn to an even more important component of efficiency: reducing their effort to grasp your message as intended. For that, we need clarity.

C

Clarity

Clarity is the intentional implementation of communicative strategies, structures and recipient-oriented modalities of expression to elucidate and faithfully transmit your mental representations while concurrently avoiding obfuscation and minimizing the recipient's cognitive load.

Did you get that? If not, don't worry—that was meant to be a joke. Everything in that previous paragraph was accurate[1], but all it really means is that clarity is saying things so that others can get your intended meaning without having to work too hard. Even better, beyond ensuring you're understood, it means doing your best to ensure that you can't be misunderstood.

Getting a little more technical, clarity is the effective and efficient transfer of meaning from one mind to another. Above all, the message must get through; it's most effective when the sender's intent is received completely, accurately and unambiguously; it's efficient when it requires as little effort and time as possible—especially on the part of the receiver. Think of clarity as the package your content comes in, which makes it both useful and easily accessible.

While clarity depends to a great extent on how your message is packaged, it is also highly audience-dependent. Their ability to understand your message depends on their existing knowledge, and also on what they need to do with what you tell them. Einstein supposedly said, "If you can't explain it simply, you don't understand it well enough,"[2] but I presume he would describe relativity differently to his grandmother than he would to an undergraduate physics class. It's the same in business communication, with its diverse stakeholders who start from different points and have different purposes for your message. The sole judge of clarity is the listener—if they think it's unclear, it is.

Clarity reduces waste in two ways: it prevents errors and reduces effort for the recipient.

The cost of misunderstanding

When vague, unclear communication leads to errors, it can be costly.

- In 1998, NASA's Mars Climate Orbiter missed its intended orbit altitude around Mars because of confusion between American and metric units in software used in a trajectory calculation, at a total cost of over $650 million.
- In 1977, two 747s from KLM and Pan Am collided on the runway at Tenerife airport, killing 583 people, partly because the KLM pilot thought he had received clearance for takeoff. When he radioed the tower that he was "at takeoff", the tower understood it to mean they were in position to take off, when they were actually rolling down the runway already.
- In 1854, the famous Charge of the Light Brigade into murderous artillery fire was caused by vague orders that sent the brigade down the wrong valley to attack the wrong target.

You or I may never be in a position where our lack of clarity can have such costly consequences, but see if any of these ring true:

- You playfully joke with someone over email, but they don't see the joke and take offense.
- You leave a meeting thinking the other person has agreed to do exactly what you asked by a specific date.
- You "clearly" explain exactly how to do something, but the other person can't seem to get it.
- You leave a meeting with your boss, and all you know is that you have to "do better".

The costs of difficulty

Many if not most of the misunderstandings cited above can be avoided if the recipient makes the effort to understand, and to clarify if they have doubts. But thinking is hard work, so many people will not make the effort, and it can cost them. As an example, studies have shown that properly used car seats can reduce infant mortality by 71%, but car seats are used improperly 79-94% of the time. A major reason is that car seat instructions are written at the 10th grade level, but the average reading level in the US is 7th grade level.[3] When people can't understand something, they quit reading, even when it's critical information.

It's easy to blame the listener for not making the extra effort to understand, but if you're sincerely striving to add value you must take responsibility.

Anything you can do to ease this "cognitive strain", as Daniel Kahneman calls it, will make your message more persuasive and actually more pleasurable to listen to.[4] As we saw earlier, Samuel Johnson said: "What is written without effort is read without pleasure." If you want to maximize your chances of getting through to the other person, keeping their attention, and getting the agreement that will benefit both parties, *you* have to do the work.

Give It to Major Brown

Legend has it that when U.S. Grant would have his staff write a battle order, he would instruct a staffer to go out and show it to a certain Major Brown.

Eventually, a staffer asked him why they bothered with that—after all, it was a security breach and it took time— why show orders to a lowly major?

Grant replied, "Well. It's simple. Major Brown is the dumbest SOB in the army, and if he can understand it, then everyone else will."

Story courtesy of Vice Admiral Cutler Dawson[5]

Transmission problems: Why we aren't as clear as we could be

If the other person does not clearly get what we intend to communicate, let's first make sure it's not our fault. There are so many influences that can degrade our clarity that sometimes it's a wonder that we can communicate at all. Some of the same factors that make us long-winded, also work against clarity, but there are other reasons as well:

Curse of knowledge: This term, which was popularized by Chip and Dan Heath in their book, *Made to Stick*, describes the fact that when we know something really well, we forget what it was like not to know it, and that makes us think it's easier for others to grasp than it actually is. We may leave out important details or assume they know what our words mean. This especially applies to jargon, because we often get so comfortable with specialized language that it becomes about as noticeable as the air we breathe.

Ego: The example that opened this chapter could easily have been written or spoken by someone with an ego problem, someone who wants to impress the listener with their intelligence, who thinks that fifty-cent words can make themselves appear to be smarter than they are.

Fear: The truth can sometimes be scary, and we might be afraid to spell it out clearly to the other person. Or, especially in these politically correct times, it can seem almost impossible to say something that somebody won't take offense to, so we deliberately use ambiguous words and phrasing that we can claim meant something else.

Confusion: We often try to express things without clearly understanding them ourselves, because what feels perfectly clear in your own mind can come out sounding like gibberish when you try to put it into actual words. Remember Einstein's admonition about simplicity.[6]

Excessive precision: You may be so afraid of being misunderstood that you go overboard. Read any legal documents to see how accuracy can sometimes be the enemy of clarity. Worse, you may seem pedantic.

Strategic reasons: There are many good reasons not to be crystal clear, often having to do with preserving the relationship. Tact is a form of strategic ambiguity, for example. And sometimes you may need to have plausible deniability, such as when you say: "You may want to think very carefully about that decision."

Balancing brevity and clarity

Waste reduction in lean communication requires cutting time and effort, but sometimes you have to find the right balance.

If you make a sincere effort to be brief, you will almost surely become clearer at the same time. First, you will strip out a lot of the excess verbiage that hides your actual meaning. Second, the extra effort you put into thinking about what you want to say will make things clearer in your own mind. It also can work in reverse, where being clear saves time, by helping others more quickly grasp your meaning

But sometimes you can be too brief and make it too hard for the other person to understand. Sometimes less actually is less. The "curse of knowledge" may lead you to cut out information that is obvious to you, but unclear to the listener. Too many explanations start out like the recipe for rabbit stew: *Step 1, catch a rabbit.* Then, you're off onto the next step of your explanation while the audience is still trying to make sense of step 1.

Brevity and clarity can correlate or clash, depending on the situation, the topic, and the needs of the audience, so ultimately you must use your judgment. The next three keys to Lean Communication will produce greater clarity and find the right balance:

- transparent logic
- candor/directness
- user-friendly language

5

Lean Communication Key #5: Transparent Logic

Call to Action
Make the logical structure of your thinking transparent to yourself and to your listeners.

Summary
If you're trying to get your listener from Point A to Point B, it helps to have a clear road map, especially one that follows the paths most familiar to them. You can improve the quality of your ideas and boost your clarity by sticking to standard logical structures and making them transparent to your listener, both in your preparation and your presentation. This chapter introduces the most important rules of structure and provides six standard structures that will be clear and familiar to business audiences.

Transparent logic
Lean thinking uses a technique called *visual control*, which is a way of communicating information rapidly and efficiently using visual signals. For example, tools can be hung on a wall using a shadow board, which simply has an outline of each tool where it belongs. That makes it easy to spot if something is missing or out of place.

Visual control is also used to lay out steps in a process so that it is obvious what happens next. As one lean practitioner put it, "If I can see it, I can fix it."[1]

Transparent logic is a means of visual control that makes your message much easier to understand by letting all parties see how all the pieces coherently fit together. That's why the first key to achieving maximum clarity is to make your logic as transparent as possible—first to yourself and then to your listener.

Transparent logic is a verbal version of an augmented reality map. Why do we have maps? To show people how to get from point A to point B in the quickest and easiest way. Whoever went first on the journey probably made a lot of mistakes and took many wrong turns before figuring out how to get to the destination, but by drawing a map of the journey they saved a lot of trouble for everyone who came after. What works for geography works for logic also. When you get immersed in a complex topic or situation, there is a mass of facts that you accumulate and gradually make sense of, before you finally arrive at your point B conclusion. By showing your mental map, you do a lot of that work for them, and illuminate the path to understanding.

The structure of your communication is a mental and verbal map that makes sure you present your ideas in the best order and that listeners don't get lost in trying to follow your logic. Just like a map, it helps you by relating what you see in front of you to the big picture; you can see where you are in the journey and where you need to go next to get to your destination. It provides a gauge of your progress, where to go next, and what to avoid.

To demonstrate, here's a map of what we'll cover in this chapter:
- How transparent logic helps
- How to make logic transparent to yourself
- How to make logic transparent to your listener

How Transparent Logic Helps

To see the benefits of transparent logic, let's go back to the economics of lean communication: the purpose is to improve the **Return** on **Time** and **Effort** of communication. Transparent logic directly enables and enhances all three factors.

Return

Transparent logic improves the return on communication by improving the quality of the thinking that goes into your idea and by ensuring that the message is received as intended.

It improves the quality of your idea by exposing the clarity (or lack of it) in your thinking. When you have a good idea to communicate, it always sounds good in your head, and you may be totally confident that you can express it that way to others. This may be the case most of the time, but you're not Superman. As Barbara Minto says in *The Pyramid Principle*, "No one can know precisely what he thinks until he has been forced to symbolize it—either by saying it out loud or by writing it down—and even then the first statement of the idea is likely to be less precise than he can eventually make it."[2]

Cognitive scientists call this phenomenon the "illusion of explanatory depth".[3] In one study, participants were told to rate how confident they were in their knowledge of how mundane things work, such as refrigerators and toilets. Most people were confident that they understood how they worked, but when they were asked to write detailed descriptions to explain them, they fell far short. And it's not just in the psychology lab—there is so much information readily available that most people tend to skim ideas on the surface, and they come away with the mistaken impression that they know more than they do.

Until you force yourself to put your ideas into some logical order, you can't be sure how well prepared you are. In my own experience, I am *always* overconfident at the beginning, and it can be quite humbling to start writing and quickly find out the gaps in my own understanding.

Without making structure transparent to yourself, it is easy to put down a lot of facts and unconnected thoughts and feel like you have accomplished something. For example, suppose you're packing for a road trip. You can throw a bunch of stuff you think you will need into the back of your car, and when it's full you will probably feel like you have everything you will possibly need. But you will never know until you get there—and when you need something, it will be too late. Don't mistake full for complete.

Structure acts as your quality control filter. Just like that shadow board, when you select a clear structure and then begin filling in the detail, you will begin to spot weaknesses in your thinking, gaps in your knowledge, and potential objections.

Transparent logic can greatly reduce the chances of misunderstanding. Our minds like order and automatically look for underlying patterns and relationships, so if we simply perform a "data dump" of loosely connected facts, your listeners may impose their own order (assuming they don't just tune out), and it may not be the one you want them to get. If you show someone an inkblot and ask them what they see, the range of possible answers is infinite. But if you ask them: "Do you see a dog in this shape?" you have already biased their minds to see the dog, and it is much more likely they will see the same thing you do.

Time

Transparent structure also saves time, both before and during the communication.

My own preparation moves much faster once I've established a clear path. In my own experience, I always have trouble when preparing for a presentation, or starting a chapter or a blog post—until I settle on a structure. Once that happens, everything falls into place much faster. It helps to show what you need to put in each place.

It saves time during the conversation because the discipline of structure will help you to be concise. When you have a clear logical structure, it becomes easier to apply the 4-I test discussed in Chapter 4. It gives you the right openings in which you can insert just the right evidence and detail that supports your points.

Finally, one reason that explanations can take longer than necessary is that you don't always know how much or how little the audience needs to hear from you, because it varies on how much they know about the topic and what their stake is in it, so you tend to err on the side of too much. When you provide a clear structure up front, it serves as a menu that they can choose from. They will tell you what they need to hear, or what you can skip.

Effort

Everyone shudders at the words, "some assembly required", because it usually entails more effort than is implied. Your listeners will appreciate a transparent structure because it reduces their effort to follow your logic. It can be hard work to follow a presentation or even an extended conversation, and most people prefer not to have to think too hard. If they have to dig the meaning out of a mass of unrelated words, they may not make the effort.

A disordered presentation is like unassembled furniture from IKEA. It's possible for the audience to put the pieces together themselves, but it's certainly easier for them if you do it for them. Besides, it's much more likely the finished piece will come out as intended!

Remember two things: first, they don't know as much about the topic as you do. What seems perfectly obvious to you now was probably not that clear at one time. In essence, you have forgotten what it was like not to know what you know now. Second, conversations and presentations are oral. Without paper, your listeners don't have the luxury of being able to re-read something that was on a previous page to connect the dots with what you are saying at the moment; they have to try to keep up. At 130 words per minute, a ten-minute presentation will contain 1300 words, which is a lot of information if it were on paper.

As Barbara Minto says, *"You must recognize that a reader, no matter how intelligent he is, has only a limited amount of mental energy available to him. Some of it will be used up just recognizing and interpreting the words, a further amount seeing the relationships between the ideas, and whatever is left comprehending their significance."*[4]

Minto was referring to the operations that go on in the recipient's working memory, which is the very limited bottleneck through which the mind absorbs new information. By providing structure, you are "adding value" by doing the second two operations for them: helping them see the relationships between ideas and comprehending their significance. In effect, by making your logic transparent you are doing their work for them.

As we'll see in Chapter 8, working memory is limited in the number of chunks of information it can handle at one time. Transparent logic clarifies things for the listener by reducing the amount of different things they need to hold in their minds as they process your message. For example, chess masters can glance at a board of a game in progress and easily remember the position of the pieces when asked to reconstruct it. It seems like an incredible memory feat, but when tested on their ability to remember the positions of pieces randomly placed on the board, they are no better than amateurs. That's because they first spot the logic, and then reconstruct the facts from that. In the same way, your listeners can easier recall your three main points than they can remember the dozen or so facts that support them.

How to Make Logic Transparent to Yourself

Before you can make logic transparent to others, you need to make it transparent to yourself. Let's look at some general rules to keep in mind when selecting a proper structure, and then examine how to make our own work easier through standard work.

Rules of structure

Theoretically, you could structure your communication in almost any way that makes sense to the listener, but some formats work better than others because of how the mind likes to make sense of information. It responds well to flow, tension and resolution, and three-part structure.

Forward Flow

A presentation or conversation that flows forward naturally just feels effortless and right.

Forward flow is about presenting your ideas at just the right pace for your listeners. Too slow and they will get distracted or frustrated; too fast and they will get confused or lost. As we see in Chapter 8, the Pull Principle addresses this challenge by putting the listener in control of the rate, but you can make it easier and more engaging for them by arranging your material so that if flows evenly and smoothly.

Strive for a smooth forward flow where there are no obvious disconnects between one point and the next. You can achieve forward flow by anticipating—and then addressing--the questions that likely will arise in the listeners' minds after every point you make.

Tension and Resolution

Everything tastes better when you're hungry, and this applies to audiences as well. Effective structures make the listener hungry by creating a need and then filling it. Problems create a desire for solutions; questions beg for answers; what's just OK drives a search for what is better. That's one reason that stories are so powerful: they introduce conflict and then resolve it, often multiple times within a larger story.

This doesn't mean that all your messages should be structured in the form of a story, with a beginning, middle, and end, but they all should take advantage of the contrast between the situation that exists and the one that you're proposing. Tension and resolution are logically at the heart of lean communication, because value is about improving outcomes. That means there is a mismatch between what *is* and what *could be*.

Rule of 3

For some reason, our minds like ideas in threes. Stories tend to have a situation, conflict and resolution structure. Even with jokes, it's usually three guys that walk into a bar—not two and not four or five. Churchill didn't exactly say, "I have nothing to offer but blood, sweat, and tears", but that's the way most people remember it.

In a sales situation, you may have five reasons why someone should buy your solution. Should you tell them all five? Although research shows that it depends on the situation, the short answer is no. When the audience is not that intellectually involved with the situation, then more reasons tend to be better. However, when the audience members are involved and are really thinking, you run the risk that the weaker reasons will dilute the stronger. If they are going to forget some of what you told them, why take the chance that they will remember the weaker and forget one of the stronger reasons?

Does it matter in which order you arrange your points?

If you have three reasons to choose your solution, does it matter whether you talk about the strongest reason first, second or third?

The answer, according to the research on persuasive communication, is "not much". The studies that have been done do not find clear differences between strongest first or last, although they suggest you should not bury your strongest reason in the middle.

However, considered in light of my own experience in presenting to senior executives, the answer is that you should definitely lead with your strongest reason. There are two reasons for this. The first reason is short attention spans. If your listeners' attention can be hijacked at any time, it makes sense to go with your strength to maximize your chances. Second, executives tend to be impatient and decisive. If they have heard enough to make a decision, they may cut you off and decide right there. This happened to me once in a presentation in St. Louis, and you can bet I did not insist on finishing all the slides I had prepared!

Standard work

In lean manufacturing, standard work means documenting the best practices of how the work gets done to establish a baseline for further improvement. Besides reducing the variability of outputs, standard work also makes it easier for new people to learn the process. The same idea can apply to communication, particularly for complex topics and long presentations.

It can sometimes feel intimidating to try to figure out the best logical structure for a large mass of data that you've accumulated, and it is hard work if you try to reinvent the wheel each time. But fortunately, just as fiction writers know that there are only a few standard plots, lean communicators know that lean conversations and presentations tend to follow one of just a few established patterns.

If you have a small library of mental templates you can make it easier to organize your thoughts without having to reinvent the wheel each time you think and communicate. It makes things easier on you mentally as well, because it reduces the number of decisions you have to make during preparation. As lean expert Dan Markovitz writes, "Jon Stewart said that it took him six years to write his first 45 minutes of material. Now, with a rigidly defined process (and, to be fair, a team of writers), he creates 30 minutes every single day. The structure and the standard work you define enable you to manage the unpredictable crises."[5]

Standard work also benefits your listeners. When they are used to receiving information in a particular way, it makes it much easier for them to absorb even complex ideas.

Here are six suggested standard structures that you may use. When you use these regularly with the same people, they will learn to expect things presented in a certain way, which can remove a tremendous amount of waste from the process.

Topical is the simplest, but can also be the most powerful. In effect, the structure is a pyramid, with the main point at the top, supported by reasoning and evidence below.
- Point: "We need to do X because…"
- Reason #1 plus supporting detail
- Reason #2 plus supporting detail
- Reason #3 plus supporting detail
- Call to action

Problem/solution structure. Many proposals are the solution to a problem.
- What is the problem?
  - Description
  - Root cause
  - Consequence
- Criteria for solution
- Alternatives considered
- Recommended solution
- Implementation plan

Opportunity/investment: If there is no immediate pressing problem to be solved, but an opportunity to be seized, you can lay it out in the way the mind considers an investment proposal:
- What is the opportunity?
- How much is the investment?
- What are the risks?

- What's the return? This does not have to be expressed in dollar terms, but the more you can quantify it, the stronger will be your argument.

SCR: This stands for Situation, Conflict, and Resolution. Also known as the story structure, it's very powerful because our minds respond well to stories. The SCR structure is not technically "lean", because it saves the punchline for the end, but it does have great flow, so if the story is well told, it can save time and reduce waste by engaging attention very well.

- Situation describes the present context or future goals,
- Conflict describes the issue that needs to be addressed and its consequences, and
- Resolution is the "happy ending".

YTT: This stands for Yesterday, Today, Tomorrow. It's useful for situation updates or regularly scheduled reviews. Here's where we started from, here's where we are today, and here's where we need to go tomorrow. It has good flow, and is useful for bringing everyone in the room up to a common level of knowledge.

- Yesterday: Describe the origins of the situation
- Today: What is the current state, and why it's not satisfactory
- Tomorrow: What needs to happen and what the benefits will be

Your Boss's Favorite Structure: No, this is not a joke. Many executives have developed their own preferred structures for receiving information with which to make decisions. You should pay close attention to the questions they ask when you or others present, and figure out the pattern they seem to prefer.

How to Make Your Logic Transparent to the Listener
Simply putting your ideas into a clear logical structure will go a long way to creating clarity and transparency for the listener, but

there are also things you can do while you're talking to ensure they follow you. It's like the difference between giving someone directions from your mental map and actually showing them the map itself.

Signal your logic up front

As we saw in Chapter 3, advance organizers can significantly boost your chances of being understood. Giving someone an outline of your logic up front works as an advance organizer in the same way that top-down messaging does.[6] As with a jigsaw puzzle, when you know the general outlines of the main objects in the picture, it's easier to place the pieces properly.

In fact, signaling your structure up front also serves as a quality control mechanism, because if you forget to cover one of the points you said you would cover, the listener will probably catch it. That's not always a good thing, as Rick Perry found out—he was the presidential candidate who said he would eliminate three federal agencies if elected, and then forgot the third. Listeners definitely caught it!

To make your logic transparent up front, you can give a quick outline of your structure at the front of the presentation or answer. In speeches and presentations, it has long been known as the first of the "Three Ts": as in "Tell them what you're going to tell them…"

For example, you could say, "I'm going to describe the problem and its implications, the criteria that any solution should meet, and then list the alternatives we've looked at, and finally my recommended solution." Another example is, "There are three reasons I think this way…the first is…"

These are both examples of verbal agendas, but of course you can show them a formal agenda as well; it could be a slide up front or a hard copy for each listener. If you do this, you'll score points with your audience by offering to add items or modify/skip some points according to their knowledge level or specific interests. For example, they may tell you they already understand the need to solve the problem, so they might want to skip right to your analysis of the root causes or your recommended solution.

Provide structure during your talk

Like a map imposed on a satellite photo, if you provide signposts and transitions that let the listener know that they are making progress, and where you are in your journey, it makes things much clearer for them and also helps to maintain their attention.

Transitions and **signposts** mark the start and end of specific topics during your talk. They give the listener a moment to orient themselves and be better prepared for the information to come next.

"My next point is…"
"To show you what I mean, here are two examples…"
"Finally…"

Highlights stress specific pieces of information. You can say things such as: "It's very important that…" "Don't forget…"

What else works? Questions make for great transitions, because if done right they track with the listener's thinking. "That's the problem. What's the solution?" If you anticipate their next logical question, you will tap into the flow that's important to them and keep them engaged.

What about summarizing?

The classic 3-Ts structure recommends that you "tell them what you told them." However, that's not always the best advice. Put yourself into the listener's position: if you got the message the first time, you would probably consider it wasteful and possibly even irritating to be reminded again what you just heard. Use your judgment: pay attention to whether the audience has received the message clearly and be prepared to dispense with your summary. If they've received the message, give them a call to action instead.

Transparent logic boosts clarity by letting others see into your thinking. That takes courage, even more so when it's fortified by our next lean communication key #6: Candor and Directness.

6

Lean Communication Key #6:
Candor and Directness

Call to Action

Always speak up when necessary to add value or prevent loss of value, but choose the appropriate level of directness to maintain effectiveness and respect the relationship.

Summary

Candor is whether you should speak up, and directness is how you should say it. You have a responsibility to be candid when keeping quiet will subtract value in the form of someone making an error. You have a choice about how directly you should say it, so that the message gets through effectively and respects the relationship. This chapter outlines strategies for when and how to dial directness up or down.

Candor and Directness

Lean communication key #6 is to tell people what they need to hear as efficiently and effectively as possible, which brings us to candor and directness.

What's the difference? Candor and directness are close cousins but are not exactly the same thing. You can be direct without being candid, and candid without being direct. When Richard Nixon said, "I am not a crook", he was being direct but not candid. When you tell someone, "you might consider a different outfit", you are candid but indirect.

The difference between candor and directness is the difference between *if* you say something and *how* say something.

Candor is a decision about content: should you say something or keep quiet? Candor is not simply honesty, it is proactive honesty—it requires you to speak up even if not asked. If you sit in a meeting and realize someone is making a mistake but only point it out if you're asked, then you're honest but not candid.

Being candid is about taking responsibility to speak up when it will improve a situation or avert a problem. In that sense, a case could be made that candor actually belongs in the value section. Since the first rule of lean communication is that it must add value, keeping quiet when you have information that could improve the situation defeats the purpose and may even subtract value, by permitting a mistake.

While candor is a responsibility, directness is a choice. You have an obligation to be candid, but you don't have to be direct. Think of candor as an on/off toggle and directness as a dimmer switch.

When should you be candid?

When should you be candid? The simple answer is "all the time," but of course that's not always easy.

Even more than directness, candor may require courage, and lack of it may be the principal reason people do not speak up when they should. In his book *Outliers*, Malcolm Gladwell tells the story of an Avianca flight that crashed in New York in 1990 after it ran out of fuel. There were a series of errors that led to this seemingly easily avoidable mistake, but one incident in the story is chilling. Because the flight had been forced to circle several times due to air traffic control problems, it was obvious even outside the cockpit that something was wrong. When a flight attendant opened the door to check to see how serious the situation was, the flight engineer pointed to the empty fuel gauge and made a throat-cutting gesture with his finger, but *neither one said anything to the distracted pilot!*

Candor is extremely valuable in business today, where constant change makes it imperative to be open about problems as soon as possible, and because the internet makes it very hard to hide information anyway. When lack of candor blocks the flow of vital information inside an organization, it can be as damaging as a blocked artery.

How many meetings have you been to where there seemed to be general agreement on a decision, only to find out that the real discussion went on after the meeting, in hallways and small groups? When candor is absent, things don't get done, problems don't come to light, and grievances fester. Problems build up unseen until they usually manifest themselves in a highly destructive and public manner. For this reason, candor is a necessary organizational relief valve.

Candor is a no-brainer when it's safe; why wouldn't you speak up to improve a situation or avert a problem when there's no cost to you? The problem is that candor often takes courage because it's risky.

In the Avianca case or the far more common business-meeting example, it's easy to fault the person who did not speak up for their lack of courage, but how often is the problem made worse by the very fact that they need courage to speak the truth? In a HBR interview, Jack Welch says, "Above all else, though, good leaders are open... They're straight with people." He then goes on to say, "...we don't understand why so many people are incapable of facing reality, of being candid with themselves and others."[2]

When Welch said he didn't understand why people weren't more candid, he perhaps wasn't being totally candid himself, as this quote from a Fortune article tells us: "Welch conducts meetings so aggressively that people tremble. He attacks almost physically with his intellect—criticizing, demeaning, ridiculing, humiliating."[3]

These two perspectives point out that leaders who want to foster a culture of candor must make it safe—or at least not job-threatening—for employees to speak their minds. Nothing is more self-defeating than hiring people for their brains and forcing them to keep quiet when they disagree. Chapter 11 covers a leader's responsibility for psychological safety in the organization.

But even when it's unsafe, (maybe *especially* when it's unsafe because no one else will speak up), if you want to be more than just a hired hand, you have a responsibility to contribute to the good of the organization or the larger purpose. WIFU has to exceed WIFM.

Candor is very much in line with outside-in thinking, because it places the needs of the listener above your own. As Warren Buffett said in his 2009 annual report, "Our goal is to tell you what we would like to know if our positions were reversed."

So, I do believe candor is non-negotiable in most situations, and I feel qualified to say that because the only time I was ever fired from a job was for my candor. When the bank where I was running the management training program got into financial trouble, they made plans to lay off 90% of the trainees upon the completion of the program. But they cautioned me one morning not to say anything because they wanted to keep as many of them around so they could choose from the best. At an all-hands meeting that afternoon, one of the trainees asked me what the bank's condition would mean to them, and I advised them to make sure their resumes were up to date[4]. I was unemployed 24 hours later, but my conscience was intact.

If you do work in a culture where candor can be dangerous, it does not absolve you of the responsibility to speak up when it's necessary, but you should definitely be smart about it. First, make absolutely sure you have your facts lined up to support your position. Second, be smart about how you speak up—that's where style comes in. Unless the situation is imminently critical (such as when your plane is about to run out of fuel), it's OK to be less direct to make what you say more palatable to the audience. If they don't take the hint, you can become more direct.

But let's not dwell just on the potential costs of candor. It can also be a valuable tool for persuasive effect. For example, the Q&A after a presentation is the best chance for the audience to see the genuine, unscripted you, and candor will make them see you as trustworthy, open and approachable. During your presentation, pointing out some of the disadvantages of your proposal can make the advantages look even better. Being candid about what you don't know can bolster the credibility of what you do know.

What about wiggle room; are there times when you don't have to be candid? Refer back to Lean key #1: it depends on the responsibility you have for providing value. You don't have a professional responsibility to try to improve every situation—when it's none of your business, it's none of your business. Or, if being candid will only hurt the other person without improving the situation, it's best to keep quiet.

There Is Something to Be Said Here

It was 1917. American forces had arrived in France to join the war against Germany, but were not yet actively involved in the fighting. The Commander in Chief of the American forces, General Pershing, made a quick visit to the First Division. Division commander General Sibert and his chief of staff were absent when Pershing's visit was announced, so the chief of operations put together a demonstration of a new method for attacking an enemy trench.

Sibert and his chief of staff arrived in time for the demonstration, and after it was completed Pershing turned to him and asked for his critique. Because of his unfamiliarity with the exercise, he flubbed it, as did the chief of staff when Pershing turned to him. Pershing was disgusted and turned angrily to his staff car to leave.

At that point, the operations chief made a decision. The young lieutenant colonel stepped forward and began explain the situation to the general. Pershing looked at him dismissively and began walking away. Then the colonel surprised everyone by grabbing Pershing's arm, saying:

"There is something to be said here, and I think that I should say it because I've been here the longest."

Pershing turned and stared at him and snapped, "What have you got to say?"

The colonel then launched into what he called a "torrent of facts" to explain the situation. Pershing did not comment on his facts, but said, "You must appreciate the troubles we have."

The colonel, figuring he was already in trouble, shot back, "Yes General, but we have them every day, and they have to be solved before night."

Pershing drove away without saying anything, and the colonel figured his career was shot. But Pershing soon brought him onto his staff, and kept him as his aide for the next five years after the war.

The colonel's name was George Marshall, who went on to become a five-star general and was the Chief of Staff of American forces during WWII.

Of course, none of us would have probably ever heard of him if Pershing had reacted negatively to his impromptu candid speech, but then we also probably would not have heard of him if he had not spoken up.

If Marshall had kept quiet, no one would have blamed him. Keeping quiet would have been the safest choice, but not the right choice. He spoke out because he had integrity, and because he took responsibility for the situation. If you ask for more responsibility, be prepared to pay the price.

Most times in your career you may not need courage to express your views, but if you do anything of importance, there will inevitably be times when you will be put to the test. When there is something that has to be said, will you say it?

How direct should you be?

If you have decided to be candid, then you must decide how direct you can be. Directness is about the how; it's a quality of communication style: when you decide to say something, you choose how to say it most effectively.

Lean communication is generally direct communication, because it takes the shortest distance between two minds. Directness is lean because it strips out waste. Directness is effective and efficient because it makes the meaning clear without excessive verbiage. Directness is persuasive because it shows and inspires confidence.

But the tendency toward directness has to be tempered by experience. We all know examples where speaking too directly has offended the listener or caused them to dig in their heels and react against what we're telling them to do. In that case, the short route runs smack into a roadblock and nothing happens—no value is added, and value may even be subtracted. If you have to apologize and ask again, that's not effective or efficient. So, sometimes the long way around is actually the shortest way to get to where you want to go.

The general rule for directness in lean communication is to be as direct as you can be to make your meaning clear, while respecting the relationship. Or let's turn that around: be as courteous and civil as you can be while making your meaning clear.

That makes directness a judgment call, and making the right call is actually a skill. Most of us are generally pretty good at intuitively figuring out when and how to dial the directness switch up or down to suit the situation, but we can do even better if we understand all the factors that can affect how the message is received. We'll start with a way to gauge the level of directness, consider the pros and cons of both ends of the spectrum, and then suggest specific strategies to guide our choices.

Levels of Directness

It's easy to say, "be direct but not too direct", but what does that mean? To answer that, it helps to have a way to gauge directness, because it's hard to improve what you can't measure. The gauge I'm going to introduce comes from research that was driven by high-profile airline disasters, which were caused in part by communication that was excessively indirect, or "mitigated" speech.

In one notable example where communication style was a contributing factor, an Air Florida jet crashed on takeoff from Washington National airport in 1982 because of ice buildup on the wings, killing all but five people aboard. Transcripts of the cockpit conversations showed that the co-pilot noticed a problem but did not address it directly. Instead, he hinted around it by calling attention to other planes:

> **Co-pilot:** *"Look how the ice is just hanging on his, ah, back, back there, see that? See those icicles on the back there and everything?"*
> **Pilot:** *"Yeah."*
> **Co-pilot:** *"Boy, this is a, this is a losing battle here on trying to deice those things; it (gives) you a false feeling of security, that's all it does."*[3]

The co-pilot probably had a clear thought in his mind, but he did not express it directly; he mitigated its expression by using less direct language. Mitigated speech is phrasing that is indirect, and it's often used because the speaker is a lower-level person who does not want to offend, or for cultural reasons. As you can see, even in a life-threatening situation, it may be psychologically difficult for people to speak as clearly as they know they need to.

But you don't have to fly for a living to become a user and/or a victim of mitigated speech; it's just as common in a business environment, where people are constantly tempted to veer from the straightest approach, as you can see from this example:[6]

```
Direct                                      Indirect

<------------------------------------------------------->

1        2        3        4        5        6
```

1. **Command** – "Strategy X is going to be implemented"
2. **Team Obligation Statement** – "We need to try strategy X"
3. **Team Suggestion** – "Why don't we try strategy X?"
4. **Query** – "Do you think strategy X would help us in this situation?"
5. **Preference** – "Perhaps we should take a look at one of these Y alternatives"
6. **Hint** – "I wonder if we could run into any roadblocks on our current course"

Which approach is the best? There is no textbook answer, because every one of those choices could be the best depending on the situation. If the organization is in serious and imminent trouble, and Strategy X is the only way out, the command may be the best. If you work in a very collegial and democratic culture and you need to cultivate consensus for something that is not an immediate problem, the hint might be the best. You can also see good reasons for any of the choices in between.

The point of introducing these six levels of directness is awareness, not precision. You don't have to parse every phrase that comes out of your mouth and try to classify it along the mitigated speech hierarchy, and you certainly don't have to memorize the six terms. But you should pay attention to your own—and others'—habitual modes of speaking, so you can make conscious choices about whether you need to dial the directness level up or down. There are good reasons for both sides of the spectrum.

Reasons to be direct

We'll start with reasons to be direct, because that is the bias of lean communication. When the message absolutely, positively, has to go through, err on the side of directness. We've already seen how not being direct can be fatal, which is why the airline industry has developed a training regimen called crew resource management to teach crew members how to speak directly to alert the captain to a problem.[7] When there is imminent danger that someone will make a mistake unless they are immediately and clearly informed, be as direct as possible.

It's tempting to be indirect when you're having a conversation about performance out of consideration for the other person's feelings, but this is a mistake, as I learned early in my sales training career. I was coaching a salesperson who had just completed an awful role play, and I tried to soft-pedal my feedback to spare his feelings. After I finished, another participant spoke up and told me I was not doing my job. Very directly, he told me in front of everyone that his colleague had performed poorly on the role play and needed to hear very clearly from me what he had to improve, or the entire session was a waste of money and time. I agreed with him, and it has influenced how I work ever since. While it may be damaging to the other person's ego, it's actually doing them a favor in the end.

Beware the feedback sandwich. One way that people are indirect in giving feedback is by sandwiching negative feedback between positive comments, something along these lines: "Jack, you are very good at identifying improvement opportunities for others, but you need to be more direct when you explain what they need to improve, and if you do that, you will be an even better coach." Out of those three bits of information, which do you think I would most likely remember? Human nature being what it is, I will be more motivated to notice and remember the positive parts. Besides, the mind is more likely to remember the first and last items in a list than the items in the middle.[8]

There's another benefit to directness, as you've already seen in lean key #3, top-down explanation. Putting your request right up front in your conversation makes it easier for the other person to organize the incoming information and makes you appear much more confident. Many people shy away from direct requests because they think they're pushy, but when you need help from someone, research has shown that direct requests are about twice as effective as you might predict.[9]

You also need to be direct at the end of the conversation, when you're confirming or locking in agreements.

As we'll see in Chapter 8, it's best to be direct as possible when answering closed-ended questions. You'll often be tempted to soften your answer by explaining it up front, but it's much less wasteful to get directly to the answer, and then add context or further explanation if necessary.

Besides these situations, you also should take into account your listener's style or preference. Cultures vary in the range of directness that is considered acceptable, and individuals within those cultures also have their own preferred styles. If you're Japanese, for example, what may seem perfectly obvious and direct to you may sail right over the head of your western listener, and you probably need to dial it up significantly, regardless of the discomfort it will make you feel.

Corporate cultures can matter as much as national cultures. If you're communicating internally you probably have a good handle on the culture, but it can be more of a problem when you're dealing with another company, such as in a sales meeting. Pay close attention to cues and if possible get an internal coach to give you some guidance.

Additionally, an individual's social style can vary depending on their levels of extraversion-intraversion and their preferences for assertiveness. Be more direct when you're speaking with drivers and expressives, and tone it down with analytics and amiables. [10]

Reasons to be indirect

Sometimes being too direct can get you into trouble, as I learned in tenth grade when a classmate was standing in front of my locker. I guess I was a lean communicator even then, and I simply said, "move". I received direct and useful feedback about the effectiveness of my style via a punch in the mouth, and I've since learned to be more tactful. In fact, most of us have learned that a little bit of indirection can make communication more effective, when it makes it likelier that the message will be well received. "Would you mind if I just squeeze by for a second to open my locker, please?" is sixteen times as long as "move", but infinitely more effective—not to mention safer!

You have to balance effectiveness and efficiency. From a lean perspective, excessive directness can reduce or even negate the intended value of the communication, so the curved path may actually be shorter than the straight. Communication between two parties requires both transmission and reception, and if reception is impaired because the other person takes offense or refuses to listen, no value has been transmitted.

And let's not forget the relationship aspect of the value equation. Indirectness for the right reasons is a hallmark of emotional intelligence. Effective communication is not a matter simply of transmitting ideas—it's also about negotiating relationships. According to Deborah Tannen[11], in any exchange, both parties are exquisitely attuned to signals regarding relative status and rapport, and the degree of directness or indirectness is one of the strongest of those signals. Tannen goes on to say that "indirectness is a fundamental and pervasive element in human communication," so you ignore it at your own risk.

The dictates of civility and common courtesy are excellent reasons to tone down the strict direct approach. It's readily apparent that common courtesy and concern for the relationship will make communication more effective, but it can also make it more efficient. On the surface, it might seem that wording things courteously might add waste. Being slightly less direct, and using words such as please and thank you may seem like drags on efficiency. But courtesy and civility are not friction, they are social lubricants which make communication flow more efficiently by making the listener more open to your message and more likely to accept it.

Keeping it civil and respectful is good for the organization and good for you as a communicator. It's good for the organization because it means that healthy disagreement and candor can flourish. Healthy disagreement is that which sparks new ideas, and makes it safe for people to express them even when they're not fully formed. If people are too concerned about being attacked for their ideas, they will censor themselves, and abort potentially good suggestions before they see the light of day. Directness that is interpreted as incivility is like the sand in the gears of discussion. It shuts down divergent thinking, and causes people to wall themselves off into heavily defended islands of opinion that won't even consider the merits of another's position.

The indirect approach can also be a smart strategic move. If you're presenting an idea to a group that you know is opposed to it, stating your bottom-line up front may just cause your listeners to shut down their listening or immediately begin forming counterarguments. In such cases, you can start with something both sides agree on, such as the common vision for the project, or values you share in common. The indirect approach can also be a useful strategy in gaining commitment for your ideas by making it the other person's idea.

When you're "managing up," it can pay to tone down your directness. Because directness is so closely tied to relative status, it can be seen as challenging to the senior person.

When someone objects to something you just said, indirectness can head off an argument. Salespeople have learned that it's much more effective and persuasive not to immediately answer objections head-on, but instead to cushion their responses. For example, if the customer says, "the price is too high," you don't just say, "Actually, it's not. It's in the mid-range for this type of product." Instead, you say, "I can see why you might think that, and in fact, that's something I thought myself at first. But when I ran a survey of comparable products, I found that costs have been trending upward, and we're actually in the mid-range."

Below is a summary to guide your choice of directness.

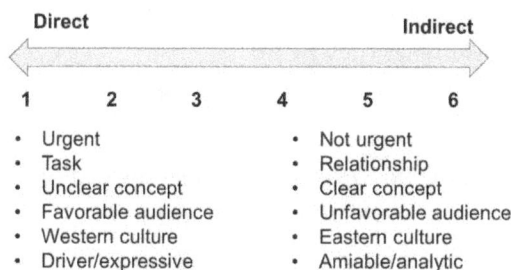

Direct	Indirect

1   2   3   4   5   6

• Urgent	• Not urgent
• Task	• Relationship
• Unclear concept	• Clear concept
• Favorable audience	• Unfavorable audience
• Western culture	• Eastern culture
• Driver/expressive	• Amiable/analytic

Intention and attention help you find the balance

Finding the sweet spot of directness could be a complex calculus, but it's simplified through two tools: *intention* and *attention*. If your intentions are guided by sincerely trying to add value and to see the situation from the outside-in, people will accept a lot of direct communication, even bluntness. Kim Scott calls it radical candor, and it's made possible when the other person trusts you because they know you care personally about them.[12] Intention is also the difference between being assertive and being aggressive: assertion is standing up for yourself while taking the other into consideration, while aggression ignores the interests of the other or even actively intends harm. If you truly have their best interests at heart, and you try to see things from their point of view, it becomes much harder to disrespect the individual—and harder for them to feel disrespected by accident.

As Tannen says, "Either directness or indirectness can be a successful means of communication as long as the linguistic style is understood by the participants."[13] That means you should pay close attention to your own style and that of the listener. In effect, it's about taking responsibility for reception as well as transmission. Many people think they're stating something very obvious, which goes right over the heads of their listeners.

- Pay attention to how the message is being received, and if in doubt, check for understanding. Going even further, you can ask them to tell you what they heard.
- Be aware of the listener's style and preference, and suit your level of directness to suit.
- Be humble about how you express yourself. Instead of: "That's not a good idea," you could say, "I may not have all the facts, but that doesn't seem like a good idea."

In summary, be as direct as you can be, but never let efficiency get in the way of effectiveness. Always keep in mind the definition of value in lean communication: "effective communication that improves personal and/or business outcomes while respecting the relationship".

7

Lean Communication Key #7:
User-Friendly Language

Call to action
Use language that is easy for your listeners to understand and remember.

Summary
What is clear in your mind can be difficult for the other person to grasp if your language is not user-friendly. Whether you do it on purpose or accidentally, it can be difficult to achieve the right balance between talking down to your listeners or going over their heads, and between clarity and precision. This chapter is about how to identify and fix the three forms of unclear language: smoke, fog, and friction.

Why does the New York Times write at a 10th grade reading level when the majority of its readers are college graduates and 80% have at least some college?[1] Because simple sells, and simple works. By keeping it simple, they capture less educated readers without losing the higher levels.

You should do the same when you communicate. Even if you work mainly with people who have at least a college degree, you might think you could get away with speaking to their education level, but think about what that means. Every time they listen to you, they have to exert the highest level of effort of which they are capable. It gets tiring, and people simply don't want to make the effort, at least not all the time. Everyone wants to get the information they need without having to work too hard.

We make people work too hard to understand us when we use any one of these three forms of language:

- Smoke
- Fog
- Friction

Let's examine each of these and figure out what to about them.

Smoke

> *"Shooting above people's heads doesn't mean you have superior ammunition—it means you're a lousy shot."*
> John Maxwell

Smoke is language that's deliberately puffed up to try to make the speaker sound more intelligent or the topic more important.

When talking to others, there's a sweet spot for word choice. Make it too simple and people get bored or feel like they're being talked-down to. Make it too complicated and people misunderstand or check out. Most of us fit comfortably in that middle ground when we talk to our friends and work peers. But something seems to happen when we address a group, or someone we are trying to impress. We switch to more formal and even pretentious language, probably because we think it elevates us or our subject matter in their estimation.

That's why we say, "Please extinguish illumination before vacating the premises," instead of "Turn out the lights when you leave." In one study, 86% of Stanford undergraduates admitted that they tried to make their papers more complex to appear more intelligent.[2]

But inflating your language to make yourself appear smarter is wrong for two reasons. The first reason is obvious but might not convince you: if you make yourself look smarter but your listeners can't understand you, you have not added any value. You've put your own goals ahead of your listeners' needs.

The second reason is somewhat surprising, and should convince you, because it directly affects how you are perceived. Despite the old saying, many people will conclude that where there's smoke, there's *no* fire! According to the same study that asked the Stanford undergrads about their writing, bigger words actually make others judge you *less* favorably. Why would that be? There could be a couple of reasons. First, it's human nature: if they don't understand what you're saying, they can either conclude that you are smarter than they are, or you don't know what you're talking about. Which do you think is more likely to happen? Also, if you're speaking with people who know what you sound like in real life, you will come across as fake, or like you're hiding something.

The best way to impress others with your intelligence is not to elevate your language, but to make your points clearly, and familiar words are your best tools for that purpose. Good writers have known this for a long time. As Churchill said, "Broadly speaking, the short words are the best, and the old words best of all."

Big, unfamiliar words are not necessarily bad; sometimes you need a special word to be precise about meaning or a certain nuance. If you're speaking with an audience that is as clued-in to the topic as you are, let them fly. With economists, for example, it's OK—even advisable—to say *disintermediation* instead of *cutting out the middleman*. Other times, it may be an aesthetic judgment: maybe a specific word pops into your mind that feels just right, even if it's just a little bit out of the ordinary. I think it's perfectly OK to use it to add an occasional dash of color. But big or esoteric words are bad when they are used to try to impress, rather than to express.

When writing down what you want to say to someone, write it for the ear and not the eye; what looks good on paper may not sound natural. I once made a cold call to a VP of Sales. After I introduced myself, I launched into my carefully crafted value proposition, which was a masterpiece of polysyllabic complexity (kind of like this). When I finished, there were a few moments of silence on the other end, until he said: "I didn't understand a word you just said!"

I apologized, and then said, "I think I can help you increase sales by at least 20%."

He replied, "*That*, I can understand!

Since that incident, I've always found it helpful to say things out loud if I have any doubts.

How to Clear the Smoke

Smoke is the easiest of the clarity problems to avoid. First, be yourself and be conversational, even when you're giving a formal presentation. Imagine that you are talking to a good friend over a beer. Warren Buffett is famous for the plain speaking he puts into his annual reports. He says he writes as if his only reader is his sister, someone who is reasonably intelligent but does not happen to know as much about the topic as he does.

Second, know your audience, to know what they know. If you have to use an unfamiliar term, define it the first time you use it, and give an example.

FOG

Have you ever come out of a meeting or presentation, and realized that you had trouble putting into words exactly what was said or decided? Maybe it's because you were blinded by the fog.

Fog has two slightly different but related meanings. As an acronym, FOG stands for "fact-deficient, obfuscating generalities", in a phrase coined by L.J. Rittenhouse in his book, *Investing between the Lines*. Rittenhouse's firm studies the way companies communicate with the investment community, and his book is full of examples of corporate messages that appear to make no sense at all when you try to figure out what they're saying. He has found that companies that communicate candidly and clearly outperform companies that do not.[3] Warren Buffett has noted the same issue, writing that, "We sometimes encounter accounting footnotes about important transactions that leave us baffled, and we go away suspicious that the reporting company wished it that way."[4]

As a noun, fog stands for any communication that is unclear, ambiguous or meaningless. It creeps into communication in several forms: excessive abstraction, euphemism, vagueness, cliché, and jargon.

Excessive abstraction

Have you ever heard someone (perhaps even yourself) say something like, "our best-in-class quality and performance provides superior value that leads to unparalleled increases in productivity for our customers"?

Try to picture each of these words in your mind. You can't, because they aren't real or tangible. There's nothing "wrong" with words like quality, performance and productivity, but you're not doing yourself a favor if your conversations don't use words that listeners can see, hear, feel, taste, or smell.

When Boeing designed the 727 in the 1960s, they could have told their engineers to design a best-in-class, high quality and high performance airplane. Instead, they told them to build a plane that could carry 131 passengers nonstop from Miami and land on runway 4-22 at La Guardia (because it's a short runway).[5] Besides making it clear for the engineers, do you suppose it made it easier to sell to the airlines? This example illustrates how helpful concreteness is for lean communication. When everyone carries a shared meaning in their heads, it reduces waste by minimizing misunderstanding and by aligning efforts.

It's difficult to write about abstraction and concreteness without being, well, too abstract. If I tell you to avoid excessive abstraction, I violate the rule. A better way to say it is: "When possible, use words that people can see or feel in their minds."

Why is that important? First, concreteness makes messages easier to remember, which is important when the recipient needs to act on the message after some time has passed. A concrete message is much easier for the mind to grip. I can give you two lists of twenty words each, the first with words such as "efficiency, morale, productivity, freedom", and the second with words like "clock, lion, ship, cup", and you will recall far more of the second list when your memory is tested.

Concreteness is actually more motivational. Charities have long known that an abstract message about famine in Africa is far less effective than a picture of a starving child. It's called the Mother Teresa effect, because she said, "If I look at the mass, I will never act. If I look at the one, I will."

Concreteness reinforces effective action, which of course is the end goal of lean communication. Ideas might begin in the mind, but action takes place in the real world of nuts and bolts, dollars and cents, blood and sweat. Being concrete and specific forces you to think through your ideas thoroughly. You can talk about capturing market share all day long, but it won't mean anything until someone figures out the concrete steps that will achieve that abstract goal.

It helps to be specific. So, for example, when giving someone feedback about their work, you can tell them they need to improve their attitude, but it won't be as powerful as telling them specifically what they did that showed a bad attitude, and exactly what they need to do to improve that perception. By the same token, you may have heard of the concept of SMART goals (Specific,

Measurable, Achievable, Relevant and Time-bound); the S and M are all about making abstract ideas concrete, and that's what makes them clear and powerful.

To demonstrate how concreteness helps, here's a concrete example. How many times have you intended to do something and then forgotten about it? I learned about a technique called implementation intentions that is almost magical in solving that problem. Instead of telling yourself that you will pick up dry cleaning after work, you tell yourself that when you leave work you will turn left before the main road and pull into the back of the parking lot and pick up your blue blazer. Instead of telling yourself that you will get the paper done by the end of Christmas break, you tell yourself that you will sit down on Tuesday morning right after breakfast and write 500 words. Implementation intentions work for me almost every single time.

Abstraction is not always a bad thing. As you become an expert in a certain field, your knowledge becomes more and more abstract. In fact, it's a form of chunking, in which many concrete details can be contained in a simple abstract idea or word. So, when you're communicating with an audience of peers who share your level of expertise, abstraction can make communication more efficient and make you more credible. However, if there is any doubt about whether all audience members will understand, provide a concrete example or illustration that helps them see what you're talking about. When Steve Jobs introduced the iPod, he didn't say it had 1 gigabyte of storage, he said you could carry 1,000 songs in your pocket.

Euphemism

Euphemism is the intentional use of terms that hide unpleasant meaning, usually used to soft-coat bad news or avoid blame. When I recently heard someone had "graduated into heaven", it took me a bit to figure out he had died.

Use your judgment and tact. Euphemism may be OK if it will

avoid offending someone you're speaking to, but when it's done to protect the communicator, it is wasteful and wrong. The following example was so egregious that it was written about in a magazine article:

> *"Citigroup today announced a series of repositioning actions that will further reduce expenses and improve efficiency across the company while maintaining Citi's unique capabilities to serve clients, especially in the emerging markets. These actions will result in increased business efficiency, streamlined operations and an optimized consumer footprint across geographies."*

Translation: *"Citigroup announced layoffs. This action will save money."*

Vague, ambiguous language

Once, I talked to some executives from a company that is a leader in its industry. To prove a point, I cited some web site quotes, and asked them if they accurately expressed their differentiators and advantages. They looked at me as if I was wasting their time: "Of course, why don't you tell us something we don't know? What's your point?"

The point was that the quotes had not come from their own web site. I had collected them from the sites of each of their next three competitors. In fact, without keeping track of the source of each quote, it would have been next to impossible to match the statement with the company.

When even the executives of the company don't recognize the differences between what they say and what everyone else in the industry says, how can they expect customers to make sense of their message, to remember what they say during their presentation, or to even care?

Sometimes it seems that business people take their communication lessons from horoscope writers who put things in very general terms so that everyone reading them is struck by how much it applies to them personally. The technique was described by Bertram Forer, who gave students a "personality test" and then, ignoring their actual answers, gave each of them the exact same descriptive passage, part of which is shown here:

You have a need for other people to like and admire you, and yet you tend to be critical of yourself. While you have some personality weaknesses you are generally able to compensate for them. You have considerable unused capacity that you have not turned to your advantage. Disciplined and self-controlled on the outside, you tend to be worrisome and insecure on the inside.

He then asked the students to rate, on a 5-point scale, how accurately the passage applied to them. The mean score was 4.26, meaning that most felt their own assessment was uncannily accurate.[7]

If it were limited to horoscope writers, it would not be worth putting in this book. But it happens all the time in business, in the form of fluffy meaningless vision/mission statements, marketing copy that customers ignore, and platitude-filled speeches by upper management, and probably in a lot of those personality profiles that companies pay so much money for.

Even when it's not intentional, it's easy to let vague, non-specific language creep into your communication. Writing expert Josh Bernoff calls them "weasel words", which he defines as, "… an adjective, adverb, or noun that indicates quality or intensity but lacks precision."[8] Words such as "some", "probably", "very", "frequently", seem to say something but will mean something different to every member of your audience. They might also indicate to an astute listener that you don't know what you're talking about.

Cliches

I'm a bit ambivalent about even including clichés as a form of FOG. In most daily conversation, you're not trying to produce a work of art or literature, so if you spend too much time trying to come up with a different way of saying things every time, that's a waste of your time and effort, especially for routine decisions.

But when you need a new or difficult decision, clichés can interfere with lean communication in two ways. First, they can affect the quality and freshness of your own thinking. If your mind defaults to a cliché when you face a new situation, you may easily overlook an important difference or novelty. It's hard to *think outside the box* or *take it to the next level* and generate *world-class results* when you stay in the rut of default thinking. In my own experience, I find that when I actively try to think of a different way to say something as I write, it can often trigger a new and different line of thought.

The second problem is the effect that cliché has on the mind of the listener—usually nothing. Just like you stop noticing familiar landmarks on your way to work, you stop paying attention to terms and phrases you hear all the time. When you hear a term enough times, you not only stop thinking about what it actually means, you may tune it out entirely.

Jargon

Jargon is another of those good news/bad news language forms. Do a web search for jargon, and almost all references to it are negative. Management professor Robert Sutton calls it "jargon monoxide" because it's a silent but deadly killer. On the other hand, jargon can actually be a very efficient way to communicate information—as long as everyone in the room is part of the same in-group. But when the audience is diverse, you can easily confuse some people, and they're not likely going to speak up and show their ignorance. The difficulty you may have with jargon is that you are so accustomed to using it, you forget that others may not be familiar with your terms.

How to clear the Fog

You have five tools at your disposal to make your language concrete and precise and SAVE it from FOG. These tools form the acronym Q-SAVE:

Quantify

Although numbers may seem like the ultimate abstraction, they are actually the best way to make something real and meaningful. You can say your solution speeds up their process, or you can tell them it makes it 17% faster, which translates to $3.4 million in additional revenue.

Story

A story is the leanest communication tool you can use, because it can pack the most power into the fewest words—as long as you select the right one and tell it right. The right story is relevant to the point you're making, and it's told without extraneous detail.

For example, if you're describing a general problem, you can add a story about a customer who had a similar problem and how your solution helped and what results it generated for them.

Analogies

By definition, analogies make the unfamiliar understandable by comparison to the familiar. They influence what we perceive and what we remember. They are useful mental shortcuts that we take when we encounter new and unfamiliar situations that require a judgment or decision. Instead of starting from scratch when we encounter an unfamiliar situation that requires a judgment or decision, we search our experience for similar situations. Analogies help us understand, organize and make sense of incoming information.

Analogies carry special weight in communicating with senior decision makers because they cut their teeth on them—the case study method used in business schools is nothing but analogical thinking on a large scale. If you can find the right analogy that resonates with them, you can shortcut a tremendous amount of detail and context and have the inside track on a favorable decision.

The most powerful analogies are from the listener's own experience, so in this example, you could compare your solution to a previous decision they made.

Visuals

The cliché "a picture is worth a thousand words" is true: despite the common misconception that people have different sensory preferences, the fact is that we are all visual. Most people nowadays use slides for their visuals, but let me remind you that you can also paint pictures in your listeners' minds with words, as Martin Luther King so famously showed us.

Examples: Examples clarify by making things real in the listener's mind, and make you more credible at the same time. As the Mother Teresa effect demonstrates, one of the best types of example is an actual person. A striking example of this is a study that found that clipping a picture of the patient to a scan made radiologists more meticulous and accurate.[9]

Friction

Friction slows down vehicles and saps the power from their engines. Friction in communication does the same thing: it's my name for speech patterns that prevent you from being as smooth and confident-sounding as you should. These patterns can reduce the value of your message and add to waste in its expression. They reduce the likelihood that people will believe your message and act on it—if someone asked you to do something, would you be more likely to agree if they sound completely confident and sure of their message?

The two forms of friction that add waste to communication and reduce clarity are hedges and filler words.

Hedges

Hedges are phrases that pull your message back from absolute, such as, *I think, maybe, it seems,* and *so on.* They can make it seem that you don't sound totally confident in what you're saying. It's common sense, but there are also numerous studies that confirm that they "lead to negative perceptions of the policy, source and argument."[10]

Hedges are not always harmful, if they are intended as such. There may be times you'll want to use them as qualifiers. Sometimes, for example, you may not want to intend or signal complete certainty. If you say, "I think we're going to make the schedule", you are raising a flag that alerts your listener that there may be risks, and they can probe for more information if they choose. The same study referenced above, showed that these "professional hedges" are not perceived poorly by listeners, and may in fact add to your credibility.

Filler words

Filler words are funny. On one hand, everyone knows that they can be a problem for speakers, and in fact they are the most-commented-on behaviors that peer coaches in my presentations classes pick up on. On the other hand, very few people realize the extent to which they themselves use them. I'm not referring just to *ums* and *ahs*; *you know, like,* and *so* are also extremely common, the latter two more so among millennials.

Filler words are not always a bad thing, so you don't have to obsess over them. By some estimates, we use filler words once every ten words, and it's usually not noticeable because they're so common—ordinary speech is infested with them. They're a normal part of two-way conversation, and in that case they're actually useful because they let the other person know you're not done with what you're saying. The problem is that when you speak to groups, they don't add anything to what you're saying, and can be a problem when they're excessive. The president of the bank where I once worked was a magnetic and dynamic speaker in small groups, but when the audience hit double digits, he would almost stutter, he had so many ums.

What does excessive mean? There's no numerical definition, but the simple rule is that they are a problem when others begin to notice them. You've probably been in that situation when listening to a speaker: if you pick up on their filler words, you soon pay attention to nothing else.

So, while you don't have to strive for perfection, it mays to ensure you keep your filler words below the level where others start to notice them. The first step is to figure out if it's a problem; you can try to listen to yourself to gauge it, or ask a colleague for their opinion, because you are usually not the best judge.

The simple advice is to become comfortable with silence— there's no need to "fill" a pause with sound. Nature may abhor a vacuum, but listeners actually don't mind it. In fact, any pause will seem much longer to you than it will to your listener, so just relax.

Of course, that's easy to say and hard to do, so if that doesn't work, the next step is to create consequences for yourself. Toastmasters International has a practice called the "ah" bell, in which a designated audience member rings a bell every time a filler word is uttered. It's tough love, but it works amazingly well. Having attention called loudly and embarrassingly to each filler word quickly primes your mind to get rid of them. I've also had success with clients who offered to pay their colleagues a quarter (or more) for every one they hear.

Besides awareness and consequences, one of the best antidotes to filler words is preparation and practice. The more you know your material, the less likely you'll find yourself searching for the next thought or the right word.

Warren Buffet's Lessons on Plain Speaking

Reading annual reports can be a lot like taking a sleeping pill on a long flight after a few glasses of wine: if it doesn't put you to sleep it will definitely befuddle you. That's why it is so refreshing to read Warren Buffett's yearly letters. His tremendous knack for candor, plain speaking, vividness and audience focus is refreshing and instructive.

Candor: Very few annual reports lie outright, but they do make it difficult to figure out the truth, especially when that truth reflects unfavorably on the leadership. Buffett's self-effacing candidness actually increases his credibility.

"During 2008 I did some dumb things in investments. I made at least one major mistake of commission and several lesser ones that also hurt. I will tell you more about these later. Furthermore, I made some errors of omission, sucking my thumb when new facts came in that should have caused me to re-examine my thinking and promptly take action." (2008)

Plain speaking: This is a close cousin of candor—you know exactly what the words mean. Buffett himself weighs in on why plain speaking is so rare:

"We sometimes encounter accounting footnotes about important transactions that leave us baffled, and we go away suspicious that the reporting company wished it that way." (2006)

Vividness: One way to keep readers from digging too deeply is to bore them; that would account for the bland, forgettable language. Buffett doesn't have that problem. He makes things vivid through analogies, stories, visual imagery and lively language.

"As we view GEICO's current opportunities, Tony and I feel like two hungry mosquitoes in a nudist camp. Juicy targets are everywhere." (2008)

Audience focused: Buffett always tries to make things as easy as possible for his audience to follow. He also makes you feel like he's chatting with you in a personal conversation, not above you from a podium bathed in lights.

"To build a compatible shareholder population, we try to communicate with our owners directly and informatively. Our goal is to tell you what we would like to know if our positions were reversed." (2009)

If Warren Buffett can demonstrate plain speaking in something so bland as an annual report, there is no reason you can't in any business communication.

D

Dialogue

So far in this book we have considered communication mostly as a one-way process, in which you form and deliver a message as a finished package for your customer, and that completes the transaction. It's now time to address the obvious fact that communication is a far more interactive and dynamic process than manufacturing.

But even in manufacturing, the process does not always go that smoothly. So many things can go wrong. You may drive up to the loading dock only to find it closed, or find that you've got the wrong product, or it's not exactly what the customer needs; or they tell you they don't have room for everything you've brought, or any one of a practically unlimited number of reasons they can't get full value from your product at that moment.

All these issues just described can happen when you try to deliver a message, and more. The truth is, no matter how hard you try, how much you think outside-in, how much you polish and re-polish your message, you almost certainly won't get it exactly right the first time. You can execute each of the first seven keys of Lean Communication perfectly and still fail to produce enough value or eliminate all forms of waste. That's because no matter how carefully you've thought outside-in and prepared exactly the message you think your audience needs to hear, the odds are against it being perfect for that particular audience at that particular time.

In fact, because you can never anticipate exactly how the other person might react, or what ideas you might spark in their minds, too much preparation and striving for precision may in itself be wasteful.

You will almost certainly have to make adjustments along the way to stay on target with your message. Just as military planners say that no plan survives first contact with the enemy, the same idea applies to communicating important or complex ideas. The listener always gets a vote, because ultimately only the listener defines value.

You need dialogue to hear the Voice of the Customer

Of course, even in manufacturing, most companies don't take such a simplistic approach; they pay attention to how their products are received. Formally, it's called the Voice of the Customer (VoC), which is simply a set of practices to capture customer feedback about their expectations and experiences so they can improve their product or service.

But listening to the Voice of the Customer is even more critical in communication because unlike manufacturing, there is no time lag between delivery of the product and the receipt of feedback from the customer. Oral communication is a *real-time* exchange of value. In other words, the "product" is being consumed at the same time as it is being delivered, and customer feedback is instantaneous. To make it even more interesting, not only is the product being consumed, it is also being modified or even completely re-created through the dance of dialogue.

So, as long as you're paying attention, you can hear the voice of the customer throughout the entire process. Even while you're talking, the listener may be sending signals that will affect your own delivery or cause you to change your message.

That's a key difference that makes dialogue so crucial: your "customer" is an active and indispensable participant in the value creation process. You might even learn something from them in return that will help you together to create more value than by yourself alone. Two or more heads are usually better than one, but only when those heads are listening to, learning from, and influencing, each other.

How does dialogue help?

Dialogue is an indispensable tool to increase value and reduce waste. It increases value by improving both outcomes and relationships.

Effective dialogue produces better outcomes by stimulating better thinking, which generates better ideas, and which are more likely to be enacted.

At the risk of using a cliché, dialogue is synergistic. That's because, as communications expert William Isaacs wrote: "...the most important parts of any conversation are those that neither party could have imagined before starting."[1] Your information plus their information can often produce a new idea or insight that would not have arisen without the mutual exchange of ideas.

Dialogue also adds value by improving relationships. Indeed, it's hard to imagine any relationship without it. People need to feel heard, and they are more likely to buy in to your idea when they feel like their point of view and their needs have been taken into account. (Leaders may especially need to be reminded of this from time to time, as I cover in Chapter 11.)

Dialogue also reduces waste, but it requires a tradeoff, in which you may have to exchange brevity for clarity. Talking things out, answering questions and rethinking on the fly are going to take more time than simply delivering a message and having it accepted, so there is definitely a short-term increase in time. But over the long term, it almost certainly saves time. As the old saying goes, if you don't have time to get it right the first time, when will you have time to do it over?

Dialogue improves clarity because it can serve as a useful quality check, where a quizzical look or a simple "huh?" can avert a costly misunderstanding. As George Bernard Shaw said, the single biggest mistake in communication is the illusion that is has occurred. How will you know if communication has occurred if you don't check for understanding?

What is effective dialogue?

First, let's say what true dialogue is not. It's not two competing monologues, it's not an interrogation, and it's certainly not a debate. It's also not a simple back and forth structure where both sides share approximately equal time.

True dialogue, of the quality I hope you strive for, is more than that. It is a *genuine and productive flow of meaning between two or more individuals who share a common purpose.*

What does *genuine* mean? It means that the flow of ideas, information and insight moves along so naturally that it feels like two minds are in synch, like both sides have figuratively moved to the same side of the desk to solve a common problem together. You feel like you're talking to a trusted friend, because you respect their competence and you sense their real concern for your interests. It's informal and professional at the same time. It's comfortable, but still contains creative tension.

What does *productive* mean? It moves the interests of both sides along, closer to an intelligent decision that creates value. While both sides may personally enjoy the dialogue, neither side loses sight of the fact that they are in the meeting to serve the interests of their employers or some bigger picture. At the same time, both sides approach the conversation in a non-zero sum and long-term spirit. To borrow a phrase from the real estate industry, it is the "highest and best use" of time for both sides.

What does *flow* mean? The ideal dialogue is a conversation that flows naturally, with very few pauses and no awkward silences. You're almost finishing each other's sentences—not in a start-stop interrupting way, but in a way that builds off of whatever the other just said, and they do the same with you. Listening is easy, speaking does not feel forced, and even the occasional silence adds to the forward flow.

It's a conversation where no one is keeping score, but in the end there is a balance of contribution that feels just right, as if each person (and by the way, it can be multiple people—not just two) got more out of the conversation than they put in.

What does *common purpose* mean? When two people dance, how do you figure out who won? Of course it's a silly question, because dancing is not about winning, and that's exactly the metaphor that applies to this type of conversation. It's about moving with each other in a sincere exchange of ideas and perspectives.

The common purpose is the creation of value through an improvement in outcomes, while respecting the relationship.

Doing battle against the problem
In 1905 there was a young bureaucrat wrestling with a difficult problem, and he decided to talk it out with his good friend. As he wrote later,

"I started the conversation with him in the following way: 'Recently I have been working on a difficult problem. Today I came to do battle against that problem with you.' We discussed every aspect of this problem. Then suddenly I understood where the key to this problem lay. Next day I came back to him again and said to him, without even saying hello, 'Thank you. I've completely solved the problem.' An analysis of the concept of time was my solution."

The young bureaucrat was Albert Einstein. Would he have figured out the problem without a creative dialogue? Probably, but it was the dialogue that provided the actual spark.[2]

Three Keys to Better Dialogue: Lean Communication Keys #8, #9 and #10. We use three tools to improve dialogue: Just-in-Time Communication, Lean Questions, and Lean Listening, which are the topics of the next three chapters.

8

Lean Communication Key #8: Just-in-Time Communication

Call to Action
Allow your listeners to dictate the pace at which they receive information from you.

Summary
One of the most important sources of waste in both manufacturing and communication is the mismatch between supply and demand. The goal in both is to deliver exactly what the customer needs when they need it, and no more. It works the same way in communication, where the bottleneck is in working memory. If you overload it, the listener can get lost and tune out; if you underload it, they get distracted.

The mismatch between supply and demand is one of the most important sources of waste in both manufacturing and communication. Ideally, supply should exactly match demand: the manufacturer delivers exactly *what* the customer needs precisely *when* they need it—not a single item more or a minute too late. This ideal state is called "just-in-time", and it's a goal that manufacturers strive for.

Of course, reality usually falls short of this ideal. In both manufacturing and communication, there can be an immense gulf between supply and demand, and this can cause all sorts of problems. Too much supply piles up inventory, and not enough supply stops production. Both sides contribute to the problem, but the solution can only come from the supplier.

The traditional mass production manufacturing approach to the problem was based on the push principle—pump out as much as you think you can sell so that you can spread costs over more units. As long as your forecasts are accurate, you can make a lot of money this way.

But if you're wrong, you may produce product faster than your customer can use it, and that incurs costs that someone has to pay for. Unused inventory piles up through the system, either in your facility or theirs, and it takes up space and ties up cash. Sure, you will probably sell it eventually, but you may have to discount it and there is always a chance that some of what you produced may never be used, especially when end users' wants and needs change.

There's a more subtle problem: when you're producing too much of what the customer does not need, there's a good chance that you'll be producing *too little* of what they *do* need. The customer might not even know they're running low in one area because the piles of irrelevant inventory hide the shortages.

But it's also risky to produce slower than the customer can use it, because that may generate a different collection of wastes: lost business, frustrated and unhappy customers, perhaps even losing their business to a competing source.

So either side of the delicate balance—produce too much or too little—subtracts value and adds waste.

The same dynamic applies to communication; it's far too common to have a mismatch between the supply and demand of information. If you deliver too much too fast you can lose your audience; if you deliver too little too late you can lose your audience.

Steven Pinker, author of *The Sense of Style,* puts the problem more poetically: he calls it the baffling-boring dilemma. Go too fast and you baffle your listener; go too slow and you bore them.[1]

You risk baffling your audience when you push information on them at your pace and not theirs, such as when you throw so much on a slide that your audience feels like they're drinking from the proverbial fire hose, or you give too much context when all they need is a yes or no or a single-point answer.

Oversupply may be even worse in communication because when people need information, it's not as if they're going to place it on a shelf for future use—they usually need it to make a decision or take action at that moment or soon thereafter. That's why information is most valuable to them when they need it, not too long before and certainly not a moment after. If you give them important information too early, they have to store in in the limited "shelf space" of their long term memory.

You risk boring them when you tell them a lot they already know. They tune out and start thinking about other things, confident that they can snap their attention back when they hear something useful—and we know how often that ends up badly!

Lean manufacturing attacks the supply-demand problem by flipping from the traditional push approach to a pull system. They base their production volume and timing on the customer's say-so, only producing what customers need when they tell them they need it. In the pull system, when a customer pulls an item off a store shelf, a signal is sent to the stock room to replenish the item; that in turn sends a signal to the distributor to supply more, which in turn generates a signal to the manufacturer to make more. For this to work, the doctrine to be followed is, "Don't make anything until it is needed; then make it very quickly."[2]

In manufacturing, it's called "Just-in-Time" (JIT), as opposed to "Just-in-Case". JIT takes a lot of hard work and innovative thinking on the supplier's part, but it can definitely be worth it. This book you're reading is a product of JIT thinking; it didn't physically exist until you clicked *check out* on the shopping cart.

Two Tools for JIT Communication

There are two tools that make just-in-time work in lean manufacturing, and both can be adapted to lean communication. They are *Takt time* and *Kanban*.

Takt time is the rate at which the customer can take in the output, and so that dictates the rate at which each unit is produced. If the customer takes in 100 units a week, the producer produces 100 units a week. Over or under that rate produces waste.

Kanban, which literally means "billboard", is a signal that is sent to the producer to tell them it's time to produce another unit. It could be a red card in a parts bin, or software-generated, but the key point is that the producer has to notice the signal and respond quickly.

Kanban is examined more thoroughly in Chapter 10. Next, we'll look at how takt time applies to lean communication.

Takt time

There is an optimal rate at which people can take in new information, and that rate depends on how much they already know about the topic, how difficult it is to understand the content (both the complexity of the material and the clarity of the message), and how engaged they are. It's also highly dependent on their individual capacity to absorb and process incoming information, more technically known as *working memory*. If you overload working memory, they will miss all or part, and possibly give up and tune out. If you underload it, they will fill the gap with a second conversation that can distract from hearing everything they need.

Overloading working memory by exceeding takt time
The human brain has an almost unlimited capacity to understand and store information, but a very limited capability to take it in. Think of your listener's mind as huge warehouse with just a small

loading dock and one or two restless and temperamental workers in receiving. If those workers get overwhelmed, they will give up. If they're not kept busy, they'll get into mischief.

That loading dock in the mind is working memory. It's the step between attention and long term memory in which you repackage the information for long term storage. But working memory is severely limited; there is only so much our minds can absorb at once, especially if we are hearing new material and concepts.

Working memory involves two operations that are critical to understanding an incoming message: taking in and connecting. We first have to take in the signals, which entails understanding the actual words heard and what they mean in this particular context, while simultaneously absorbing the nonverbal signals that come along with them. That's akin to the process of taking the incoming product and getting it into the door of the warehouse.

Next, we have to connect the information to something that we already know. Sticking to our warehouse analogy, the workers in receiving have to figure out where to put the incoming product. For example, if someone says they saw a green dog, we would presumably know enough about dogs to be surprised by the information. If someone says they saw a green frimfram, we may not know enough about frimframs to know what to make of that statement. For a more practical example, if someone says that revenues increased by 10 million dollars, it only makes sense to us if we know at least roughly what previous revenues were, or what the revenue target for the year was, or how much revenues changed for a competitor, and so on.

Working memory is more than just short-term memory; it entails not just temporarily storing information but actively processing it. It's more like a mental scratch pad, where we take in information and make sense of it before it goes into our long-term memory. Any new information has to be actively processed on this scratch pad, but the pad is severely limited both in capacity and duration.

The common belief, based at least partially on a paper written by George Miller in the 1950s, is that we can hold 7 "chunks" of information in working memory at one time, plus or minus 2. A telephone number is a good example. If you're told a number and you don't immediately begin repeating it in your mind, it will generally be gone from memory within 12 seconds.[3]

However, subsequent research has shown that the actual number of chunks we can actively process at one time is much lower—ranging from two to four. For example, if I ask you to add 24 + 17 in your head, you probably won't have too much trouble. If instead I asked you to add 247 + 175, I might start overloading your working memory, because as you are adding the digits in your head you are also trying to remember the numbers I gave you.

Any time we've struggled to keep up when someone has spoken too fast or projected a slide overloaded with text and numbers, we've known what it's like to have an overflowing working memory. For example, if you're reporting quarterly financial results, your listeners must first understand the reported numbers, perhaps comparing these to their memory of the previous quarter or to their expectations, then tease out the differences between income and cash flow, and consider the implications for the next quarter. There's a lot going on in their minds, and meanwhile you've moved on to the next slide, which they then have to struggle to catch up to, until at some point they just quit trying, like a dog that realizes it won't catch the bus.

It's the same way with receiving qualitative information. When your learners receive information from you, they are not simply trying to remember the data as if it were a phone number. They are actively processing the data: contrasting it to what they already know, comparing it to other ideas, and considering its implications for their situation. Working memory is why the phrase, "drinking from a fire hose", often seems so appropriate.

Chunking information

With such severe limitations on working memory, how is it possible to communicate so quickly and to accumulate so much knowledge? It's the magic of "chunking". We progress in our knowledge of a particular topic by chunking bits of information together, so that the new combination then becomes just one piece of information to remember. For example, how easy do you suppose it would be to remember the following string of numbers?

1941177618652001

As individual numbers, most of us would be hard pressed to memorize these without spending a lot of time. But let's look at them as dates in American history:

1941 1776 1865 2001

It's much easier, right? Of course, if you do not have a strong knowledge of American history, this won't work—hence the importance of knowing your audience and starting with what they know, not what you know.

Chunking is the magic work-around to working memory limitations. We saw in Chapter 5 how chess masters could glance at a board in mid-game, and then re-create it easily from memory, while novices might remember just a few of the correct positions. But here's the kicker: when the pieces were randomly placed on the board, the experts did no better than the novices. The experts don't have superhuman memories; they just have much bigger chunks already in their minds, so they might be able to see the whole set of black pieces as one or two chunks.[4]

The idea of chunking also relates back to the problem of excessive abstraction discussed in Chapter 7. As we become more expert in a particular area of knowledge, we organize that knowledge in ever-larger chunks. Increasing abstraction is essentially the same as using larger and larger chunks.

Here's how it applies to business communication. If I tell you that we need to reduce capex by 10% this year without affecting Project X, you might see this as just three chunks of information. On the other hand, if you don't know accounting terminology, and you are unfamiliar with Project X, it might take me a complete set of instructions to impart the same information.

But there's the rub: if I don't know how much you know already, there's a possibility that I will use chunks that you don't yet understand; in fact, because of the curse of knowledge, it's more likely that I will assume you know more than you do. So, when you hear a term or concept you don't fully understand, you're going to have to use some of your limited working memory to try to figure out what it means—and while your mind is occupied doing that, I obliviously continue talking, thinking that what I said was obvious.

As the receiver of the unclear information, you can of course stop me and ask for an explanation, but that's not a common response, because your own ego may prevent you from admitting that you didn't get it.

Underloading working memory

Clearly, it's important not to supply information faster than your audience can absorb it, but what happens when you go too slow?

Standard American English speakers produce about 125 words per minute, but we process words mentally at least four times as fast (and flashes of insight and intuition may be orders of magnitude faster). While that should make it easier to follow what the other person is saying, what happens instead is that we usually fill that excess bandwidth by listening to the "second conversation" that we have with ourselves while someone is speaking.

It's extremely difficult to avoid the second conversation during a dialogue. When the other person speaks, we listen to their words, and at the same time we listen to ourselves: our reactions, impressions, questions, or rebuttals that spring unbidden into our minds in response to their message. Or we think about something totally unrelated to the conversation, maybe an errand we need to run later, or wondering what the special will be today in the cafeteria.

That second conversation can hinder understanding, because we truly can't carry on both conversations at once. Even if it's momentary, we stop listening to the other person long enough to hear ourselves—but sometimes we don't revert to the first conversation in time, and miss something that was said. Or, we automatically assume we know how the sentence is going to end, and begin forming our response, and we miss the zig where we expected a zag.

Besides making it easier for your listeners to get bored or distracted, another danger is that you can also sound unsophisticated or even condescending if you make it *too* simple.

So it's obviously difficult to find the sweet spot between baffling and boring your listener, and of course it's even worse when you have a room full of listeners, each with a different level of knowledge about the topic. It's a wonder sometimes that any effective communication happens at all!

JIT Remedies

JIT communication may seem like a difficult target, but everything we've covered so far can take you a long way towards realizing it. To review:

- Knowing your audience will help you narrow down the sweet spot between too much information and too little.
- Answering the question makes it easy for the audience to know what they will need to get to that point.
- Top-down organization sets the context that helps them absorb

the incoming information and figure out which pieces they need to complete the puzzle.

- The *so what* filter makes your detail more meaningful to the recipient.
- Transparent structure helps them orient themselves where they are going to effectively organize the incoming detail.
- Directness and user-friendly language make it easier to understand your message, hence speeding up the input.

These lean practices are a necessary start and will get you in the right ballpark, but of course it's no guarantee that you will find that sweet spot between baffling and boring, called Just-In-Time Communication.

The only way to deliver JIT is to let the audience dictate the optimum flow of information. That means you have to pay attention to signals and respond appropriately. They may not know the word Kanban, but they certainly understand the concepts, and will almost automatically send useful signals.

Some signals are obvious: someone stops you and asks for clarification, or impatiently urges you to tell them something they don't know. It's the less obvious signals you have to watch for, because people may be too embarrassed to tell you they're getting confused, or too polite to show their boredom.

So you've got to encourage them to use the pull principle. Put your listeners more in control of the dialogue by making it easy and acceptable for them to ask for more or for less.

The pull principle adds value because the listener tells you what they need to hear to get value from the conversation.

The pull principle can also significantly reduce waste because they will only ask for the information they need to receive value. It also saves time because often they reach the point where they are satisfied with your reasoning and they will stop you.

Pull shows respect for the individual, because it assumes that they know what they need and what's important.

Pull is especially helpful when you have a diverse audience. People will assimilate ideas at different rates, and only they can tell you whether they are getting it.

Let's see how to practice JIT in conversations and in presentations.

JIT in conversation

Lean conversations tend to be question-driven, because it's the listener who defines value, and they will probably have a lot of questions before being satisfied that they are getting it. You can add value and improve the relationship if you let your listener take the lead and tell you what they need by asking questions.

Let's say, for instance, that you approach your boss with a problem and a suggestion for its solution. You will probably start with the *what* and the *why* of the conversation, and then, assuming you don't get questions immediately, begin your explanation.

In other words, establish the purpose of the conversation, and then let the other person ask you for what they need to achieve the goal. Let them pull the information out at the appropriate flow by asking questions and then respond to the question that was asked.

Many people find this difficult to do, because they might not like the questions that are being asked, or may consider them not germane to the topic. But that's inside-out thinking, putting your own needs and concerns over those of the listener. You must accord them the respect of assuming that they have a good reason for the question.

While you're speaking, you can actually send kanban signals of your own by using qualifiers and "flags" that will invite them to follow up if they choose. For example, you might say, "Under current assumptions, we should make the schedule." "The two most important risks are…" If they want to know more about the assumptions or the risks, they will ask.

It's also helpful to pause occasionally. Don't be afraid of a little silence: there is no need to fill every available second with sound. Pauses allow the listener to absorb your message, and often, just being quiet for a few seconds can get the other person to say something else. Pay extra-close attention to what comes out of their mouth to fill the silence; there's a reason it came out.

The measure of value in this case is obvious but not always honored: *Did you answer their question?*

How we get answers wrong and what to do about it
While it may seem obvious that you should answer the question, it's surprising how many people don't actually do that, at least not at first. In fact, this is one of the most common complaints I hear from executives when we discuss the reasons they may need to hire me to teach lean communication. They ask what they think are straightforward questions and get evasions or irrelevancies in return, or they get the answer but it's so buried in detail that it's hard to ferret out.

There could be several reasons for this. Sometimes people are afraid of the honest answer—they might fear the consequences of giving the person news they don't want to hear. They may think the other person is off track with their question, so they answer the question they think the person should have asked. They may be more interested in pushing their own agendas than in helping the questioner with theirs. They may not be clear in their own mind what the answer is, and they think aloud to try to get to it.

Let's see some examples:

Q: Is this a good idea?

A: Wow, that's a tough question. There are a lot of factors we need to consider. On the one hand, it's something the customer asked for, and within reason we want to keep them happy, but it is going to mean a one-time cost, which I suppose we could justify as an investment because it would help us with some other customers as well...

Q: Will the project finish on time?

A: Are you aware of how hard we've been working the past few weeks? We've been doing the best we can, but we also had to deal with the fire-drill from... With all that, I think it's quite an achievement that we're only going to be delayed little bit...

Did you get all that?

So, the first step in answering the question is to listen to the question, and decide what kind of answer is required.

If it's a closed-ended question, it may just need a simple yes or no, or a specific data point, such as a number or a name. Sometimes that is all you need in your answer, although it's often more natural to anticipate their next obvious question. For example, is someone asks if the project will finish on time, you might say, "No, but we expect to deliver by the following week." Or, if they ask how long the project will take: "Nine months, which is slightly below average for this type of work."

But pay attention to the structure of those two examples: regardless of what additional information your answer contains, the core answer is always first.

Let's try the two example questions again:

Q: Is this a good idea?

A: Yes.

Or,

A: Yes, because it will keep a good customer happy and improve our offering in the long run.

Q: Will the project finish on time?

A: No.

Or,

A: No, it's delayed by two weeks.

Q: Where is customer X in their decision process?

A: I don't know.

Or,

I don't know, but I'll call the buyer and get back to you this afternoon.

4 + 2 Ps of Answering

In this situation, you can apply the *4 + 2 Ps of Answering*.

Before	**Prepare**
During	Pause
	Point
	Prioritize
	Pull
After	**Practice**

Let's start with the middle four Ps, which describe the process in the moment:

Pause

Conversations are not game shows: you don't win prizes for the fastest answers. In fact, a brief pause before answering may make you appear to be more thoughtful, and more importantly, it will allow you to actually *be* more thoughtful. (Unless it's a very simple question; then, too long a pause may make them feel like you're hiding something.) That's because even a second or two is enough time to choose a better response. A single second's thought can mean the difference between reacting and responding, or between reflex and reasoning. As we've seen, one of the reasons that people ramble on is that they begin speaking before they have fully formulated the thought, so the answer comes out "half-baked" and needs to be modified after the fact. You can do a lot of thinking in a brief pause, especially to select your main point.

Point

Get to the point immediately. This is just a fancy way of saying that you should answer the specific question *first*. Many times, the answer being sought is a single-point answer, either yes/no, or a specific bit of information, such as a number. Even if you have reasons to hedge or refine your answer, you should give the answer first, and then hedge afterward if necessary.

How the US intelligence community handles yes/no questions

Suppose someone asks you if it's a good idea to do something; it's a simple question, isn't it? Yes/no questions would seem to be easy to answer, because there are only two possible answers, but they are actually fraught with danger, at both ends of the spectrum.

On the one hand, you may be reasonably certain that something is a good idea, but you know there are certain possible but highly unlikely scenarios in which it's not—or vice-versa. If you're excessively cautious or pedantically precise, you might be tempted to hedge your answer with every possible qualification you can think of. The problem with this is that precision gets in the way of practicality, and you may give the other person much more than they need. Besides using up time unnecessarily, there is a real possibility that your answer could get lost amidst your explanations.

The opposite end of the spectrum is what I call the binary trap. Answering a closed-ended question does not mean that you have to get boxed in to a binary yes/no choice. Real-world questions are seldom closed-ended, because the answers may depend on a complex range of factors, or depend on unpredictable factors, or we have incomplete knowledge. Even if you're unsure, you can fall into a trap of trying to give a yes or no answer to avoid looking wishy-washy, which may give an erroneous impression to the questioner. Or the questioner might be acting like a prosecutor, trying to trap you into an incriminating answer without the chance to offer mitigating information.

Theoretically, the range of possible answers to a yes/no question could be infinite, but this range is (probably) sufficient for effective business conversation.

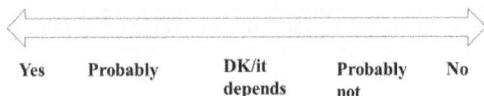

$$\longleftarrow \qquad\qquad\qquad\qquad \longrightarrow$$

| Yes | Probably | DK/it depends | Probably not | No |

(In the figure above, DK stands for "don't know".)

Having this expanded vocabulary to answer yes/no questions benefits both sides of the conversation. It protects you and allows you to explain your thinking; it also can serve as a red flag alerting the questioner that they may need to probe for more detail before they make a decision.

However, regardless of which of the five possible answers you choose, the key is to *begin* with the answer, and then add an explanation if necessary.

Q: Is this a good idea?

A: Probably. It depends on whether we can get the costs down another 10%, and we should know by next Friday.

Prioritize

You may have a lot to say in response. For example, if they ask you why you think a decision will pay off, you may have five reasons to think the answer is "yes". Prioritizing means trying to give the most important reason first. This is not as difficult as it seems, because if you have thought of your main point, there is a reason your brain came up with that answer, and even just a moment's reflection can help you pull it out.

Am I advocating talking in bullet points? Yes, for three reasons:
- It distills your thinking to easily digestible points
- It shows your logic (Lean Key #5)
- It serves as a quality check. If you say you have three reasons, they'll know if you forgot one.[5]

Let's take it one step further. Although it adds another level of difficulty to the process, you can add even more value by telling the other person how many bullet points to expect: *"There are three reasons...It depends on two things..."* Or, if you have more than three, you can say, *"There are several reasons, but the most important one is..."*

Pull

Staying on the previous example, it might be good enough to provide the first one or two reasons, and let your listeners pull others out of you if they choose to. You can let the questioner lead the conversation by paying attention to their non-verbal responses, and then checking for understanding if you're not certain whether they're getting it.

These first four Ps describe the way to answer the question during the actual conversation. The next two Ps take place before and after.

Prepare for their questions

If you're going to rely on signals from your listener to tell you what they need to know, the onus is on you to deliver when they do. You might be able to think fast on your feet, but you can always do better if you take the time to prepare and anticipate their questions.

It may be as easy as taking a few minutes to jot down the top two or three questions you think the other person will ask, or it can be as elaborate as sitting down formally with a team to brainstorm all the possible concerns and questions your audience may have. You need to decide how much time you can devote to anticipating questions, but in my experience it has always been better to be prepared and not need it, than the other way around. If nothing else, the well-earned sense of confidence that proper preparation gives you, will shine through in your conversations.

Anticipate depth, breadth and height of questioning

Superficial knowledge of your material may be just enough to get you into trouble. Be prepared for *depth*; your listeners may drill down to help their own understanding or possibly just to test you. *Breadth* refers to related issues that may come up. For example, if you're presenting an idea that could solve a specific problem, they might ask you about other problems. *Height* refers to those questions that you might normally consider "above your pay grade", but which they may ask you just to test your ability to take a more strategic or long view. How does your idea or proposal fit with the bigger picture?

Pressure-test your ideas
Research and analysis are not enough—you've got to test your position against challenges for maximum confidence. Ideas are like organisms: survival depends on adapting effectively to competition. Carefully consider the position of the listener, think of their counterarguments and then write down effective responses. Expose weaknesses and shore them up, and then enlist others to try to pick holes in your position. Depending on how bulletproof you want to be, you can even think one or two steps beyond and anticipate their follow-up question to your answer.

Practice
A funny thing happens in my Lean Communication workshops when I have participants practice answering briefly. Participants break into small groups and practice answering in five-minute rounds. The early minutes of each round are always quieter than the later minutes, because answers tend to get longer towards the end of the round. That's because keeping it lean is hard work at first.

The good news is that with a bit of consistent practice, the 4 Ps can become a habit, and you will naturally follow the process without straining to think about it.

JIT in Presentations
JIT becomes even more important as your audience size grows because there are usually more people involved so the waste is multiplied by the number of participants, and because the diversity in perspectives and knowledge levels increases the odds of a supply-demand mismatch.

To apply JIT effectively, here are some suggestions, for before and during your presentation.

Before the presentation

You can begin attacking the problem even before you show up for the presentation. Many organizations encourage people to send the presentation or any relevant information ahead of time, so recipients can read it, orient themselves to the material, and prepare their questions for the speaker. Even if it's not likely that everyone will read it, it can help if even one or two have read it before.

A lot of waste may arise when one person becomes the bottleneck during the presentation because they are not as familiar with the topic as everyone else. You can mitigate this risk by leveling the playing field before the day of the presentation. Speak to them beforehand to bring them up to speed.

At the start

Be transparent about your objectives. If they know what your "ask" is, they can decide what they need to hear. Give them the "executive summary" and invite comments.

In a little more detail, your agenda or description of the structure of what you're going to say will also help. A related way to do this is to use the tried-and-tested "tell them what you're going to tell them" approach.

Make sure that they know that it's OK to interrupt. If you're presenting upwards, you probably won't have too much choice anyway, so learn to embrace interruptions and questions. They tell you that the person is engaged, and they indicate which areas need to be stressed over others.

During your talk

Limit your evidence

If you try to pack in everything you know, your listeners will forget some of your points when it comes time to decide, and there is a danger that they will forget the stronger ones and remember the weaker. In effect, the weaker facts dilute the strength of your persuasive cocktail. Try to stick to the Rule of 3. It's a comfortable number of chunks that your audience can process at one time in their working memory, and it has a certain aesthetic appeal to their minds.

If you're hesitant to omit something you think you might need, remember that you still can rely on the pull principle. Put it in your backup slides or keep it in reserve in case a question comes up. This is helpful when you have a diverse audience and you're not sure which arguments will resonate.

Take words off slides

Besides making your slides too cluttered, there's a tendency when you have too many words on the screen to feel like you have to address each one.

Be prepared to take shortcuts

There is no ironclad law that says you have to cover every single point you prepared for the presentation, or show every single slide. Pay close attention to how your message is being received. If you're describing the consequences of not solving a problem, and you can tell everyone agrees and is impatient to hear your solution, jump right to that section. That's the value of showing your structure early in the presentation. And don't talk past the close: when you have agreement, shut up.

Pay attention to your audience

Monitor their reactions and ask questions as you're explaining to check for understanding and agreement. If you're getting puzzled looks or signs of disagreement, figure out what's going on. Do this by using questions and listening, which are the subjects of the next two chapters.

9

Lean Communication Key #9: Lean Questioning

Call to Action
Ask better questions to improve the delivery and reception of your own message, and to help the other person be more lean in their own communication with you.

Summary
Questions can be one of your most important communication tools. They help both sides work together to create more value, and also improve relationships. You can use questions to reduce waste by helping the other person formulate their own thoughts and expression more concisely and clearly. Lean questioning can also be used to reinforce the effectiveness of each of the other lean keys.

Why Questions?
Imagine you've done everything right that we've covered so far: you've crafted and delivered a message that improves outcomes and relationships, and you've made it brief and clear. That may seem like a good result and therefore a triumph of lean communication. But if the communication is primarily one-way, there is no way to tell if there might actually be a lot of hidden waste, which may take several forms:

- There might have been an even better idea left unexplored
- The relationship may have been improved even more
- What was agreed might have been interpreted differently by both parties
- The decision may not be carried fully through completion

From a lean perspective, questions are essential because there is one major area in which the communication-as-a-manufacturing-process metaphor breaks down. Your initial delivery is rarely a finished product. In manufacturing, one takes in inputs, applies work to them, and produces a product that adds value. But in spoken communication, value is added real-time, and it usually requires input and collaborative work by both parties simultaneously. Questions are the essential tool for working together to create value and prevent waste.

Except for the simplest of topics or situations, it's almost impossible to imagine any productive conversation that does not include questions. Without asking questions of the person you're speaking with, how can you be sure that they got the message as you intended? How can you be sure they agree with you? How can you gauge the state of the relationship? How can you tell if they perceive value in your message? How can you work together to improve your idea? How can you effectively send the message that you care what they think?

Every one of us knows how to ask questions—we've been doing it virtually since the day we learned to form coherent sentences. But, just like speaking or listening, there is a certain level of skill that can make you a more effective communicator. You've heard the old saying that there's no such thing as a stupid question? That may not be entirely true, but let's just say that some questions are smarter than others—smarter in that they may be more effective for accomplishing your purpose.

Questions improve the effectiveness of lean communication on both sides. So far, we've approached lean communication from the perspective of you as the initiator of the discussion, but it can be just as important if someone is trying to get you to decide or act. Unless they're already lean communicators, you may need to use questions to help them express their thoughts better.

There are entire books written about asking questions,[1] so this chapter is not going to attempt to distill all that wisdom into just a few pages. Rather, I will look at questions through the lean lens.

How can questions make communication leaner?

Looking at the big picture, communication is a process that takes in inputs, adds work (thinking) to them, and produces a valuable outcome. Questions may be needed to ensure you're getting the right inputs; thinking about them correctly (applying work in the right way); and serve as quality control to ensure that the "customer" gets value from the output.

Questions can help you add value and reduce waste in conversation. More specifically, they contribute to both dimensions of value—outcomes and relationships; they can reduce waste by cutting through excess verbiage; they can clarify meaning for both parties; and they can encourage and improve dialogue. In effect, questions can act as "force multipliers" for each specific element of lean communication.

Start with a questioning mindset

There's a skill to asking effective questions, but probably the most important asset for lean questioning is the right mindset about asking questions. That's because others' perception of your intent will significantly increase their willingness to respond and hence the quality of the answers you receive.

Humility: Humility helps your questioning in two ways. Without humility, you're unlikely to ask many questions at all, either because you think you already know what you need to know, or because you're afraid of appearing ignorant to the other person. The second reason is the effect it can have on your counterpart. Your humble desire to find out what they know elevates them into a "one-up" position and makes it more likely that they will be forthcoming with information.[2]

Curiosity: People will put up with a lot of questions if they think you have a genuine curiosity to know the answer, rather than testing them or trying to show how smart you are. Besides, curiosity will drive you to probe a little deeper or further when they do tell you stuff, and often what is said after the initial statement or answer can be very revealing. A corollary to curiosity is that you should listen to their answers not to judge, but to learn, and possibly improve the message.

Use Questions to Add Value

As we already know, the value realized from communication is a function of improved outcomes and relationships. To that end, questions can contribute added value in five ways:

1. Develop and fully understand the need
2. Assure you have the most accurate and complete inputs
3. Improve the quality of joint thinking
4. Drive action
5. Support the relationship

Develop and fully understand the need

You will recall from Chapter 1 that value begins with an in-depth understanding of the other person's needs, which requires knowing as much as possible about: a) where are they now, b) where do they want to go, and c) what's keeping them from getting there?

But even if you think you have those answers, your listener is the ultimate judge of whether they received value, so you must be receptive to their voice to know what will be most valuable to them and how they react to your idea. No matter how well you have prepared and think you have the answers, it's still at best a hypothesis until you test it, validate it, and possibly improve it. Questions are your instruments to test your hypothesis.

The questions you may need to ask, to fill in your unknowns and validate your perception of the need are the same ones from your research and preparation phase:

Where are they now?
- What do you know and don't know about this proposal?
- What is your attitude towards what I'm proposing?
- What concerns do you have?
- How do you see the situation?
- Do you see it the same way I do?

Where do they want to go?
- What organizational goals do you support?
- How are you measured?
- What's important to your department or function?
- What are your personal goals and aspirations?
- Why is this important to you?

What's keeping them from getting there?
- What *problems* do you have?
- What *opportunities* do you see for improvement?
- What *changes* are you having to adapt to?
- What *risks* concern you?

Assure you have the most accurate and complete inputs
Assuming you sufficiently establish the need, the next step is to ensure you have sufficient information to make an informed decision on what to do about it. You can use questions to improve the idea by enabling correction, addition, deletion, modification, or

synthesis. It's like putting together a jigsaw puzzle in which both sides have some of the pieces going in, and together they may be able to supply the missing pieces.

- What am I missing?
- What else do we need to know?
- How confident are we in the data we have?
- Where and when was the data gathered?
- Who gathered the data?
- Do you have any disconfirming information?
- What other sources have you considered?
- What assumptions are we taking for granted?

Improve the quality of joint thinking
Input questions can help you supply missing pieces for your puzzle, but if you stop there, you may be leaving value on the table. You next need to process those inputs through your thinking. Questions can "elevate the cognition" of all parties by improving three types of thinking: critical, analytical, and creative.

Critical thinking is a necessary start, because it's important to avoid errors. (Think of it as Hippocratic strategy: "First, do no harm".) Asking input questions to ensure that you have accurate, relevant and complete information is part of critical thinking. Critical thinking questions the inputs.

However, critical thinking is not enough. In fact, critical questions are usually the easiest to think of, because of what management professor Jeffrey Pfeffer calls the "smart-talk trap."[3] People like to show off their intelligence by poking holes in the ideas of others, but it can take greater intelligence—or at least a different form of intelligence—to find ways to positively improve their ideas, by spotting what isn't being said or thought about, or imagining additional possibilities.

Analytical thinking is used to break down and examine the

interrelationships between the facts to ensure that they make sense logically, and that they justify the conclusions being stated or implied. You can use questions to examine cause-and-effect relationships, deductive and inductive reasoning, and comparing and contrasting. Analytical thinking questions the logic.

- What do we do with the information?
- Does it make sense?
- How can we apply this?
- How does this compare to…?

Creative thinking is about putting the information and ideas together to form something new. Use questions to invite different perspectives, diversity of thought, and inspire imagination.

- How can we make something better out of it?
- What are other ways we could solve the problem?
- What would the ideal solution look like?
- Who has a different viewpoint?

Drive action

Decision makers have scarce resources and more needs clamoring for their attention than the one you're addressing, so even if they agree they have a problem and you have a good solution, there is no guarantee that they will actually do something about it. We may need questions to confirm agreement, develop the consequences of inaction, or elicit their intentions.

The most obvious but often overlooked questions to drive action are confirmation questions—what salespeople would call closing questions. We often overlook them because we might assume that we have agreement just because they haven't disagreed; or we might be afraid to ask them for fear of hearing a no. Sometimes getting a yes is the easy part, but we do have to ask:

- Does that sound OK?
- Are you on board?

But the problem with these types of closed-ended questions to confirm agreement is that it's too easy for the other person to say yes and not mean it. Maybe they're afraid to say no, or don't want to hurt your feelings. It takes a bit more self-confidence, but you might want to ask the question in a way that invites them to share their concerns. It's scary, but better in the long run.

- What concerns do you have?
- What am I missing?

What if you ask a confirmation question and get a no? Perhaps, despite all your best efforts at expressing great reasons for them to act, they're still not sufficiently motivated. That's where consequences questions come in. Consequences questions are follow-ups to your needs questions that get the other person to focus on the cost of not acting.

- What impact does that have?
- How does that affect customer satisfaction?
- What's the cost of a day's delay?
- If that happened, how would it impact _____?

The third type of action-generating questions get the other person to take ownership of the decision. People are much more likely to follow through on ideas when they feel a personal stake in it. Ask questions to get them to:

Suggest a course of action:
- What are the next steps?
- Who else do we need to involve?

Elaborate on the benefits of acting:
- How would it help if…?
- What other benefits do you see?

Articulate their implementation intentions:[4]

- What specifically will you do by when to make sure this gets done?
- Who else do we need to get involved?

Support the relationship

The mere act of asking good questions should support the relationship, because it shows you respect the other party's point of view, and you're humble enough to admit you don't have all the answers. In addition, questions are a low-key way of embellishing the relationship by supplying the important social gifts of attention, respect, and validation.

You can also ask "affective" questions to figure out their intrinsic needs and bring to light their emotional reactions to the matter at hand, for example:

- How did it make you feel?
- Are you happy about that?
- How is this affecting you?

Just keep in mind that affective questions can feel more personal and possibly intrusive to the other person, so ask them judiciously.

Use questions to reduce waste

Chances are, many of the people you speak with on a regular basis are going to be more verbose and less clear than they could be. You can use questions to reduce communication waste by helping the other person be brief in their communication with you, and to ensure you clearly get their meaning.

Questions to promote brevity in others

To promote brevity in others, use questions to apply the same keys you apply to yourself: top-down explanation (BLUF) and the So What filter. Also, be aware of the types of questions you ask.

Top Down
If someone begins rambling and you don't see their point, ask them questions to help them bring the bottom line up front (BLUF).
- Where is this going?
- Why are you telling me this?
- What are we trying to achieve?
- What decision do you need from me?
- What do you want and why?

So What?
Question the relevance or the thread by asking *so what*, but not necessarily in those exact words. Unless you have a comfortable relationship with the other person, the very question: "So what?" can sound accusatory or demeaning. But there are gentler ways to accomplish this:
- How does this relate to the main question?
- Where is this going?
- How does that relate to _____?
- Are we getting off track?

Some tips for producing briefer answers
Ask more specific closed-ended questions. Although a lot of voluble people don't take the hint, closed questions tend to produce shorter answers. Closed-ended questions seek either a binary yes/no answer or a single point of data, such as a number or a specific choice, such as, "What kind of car do you drive?"

If you're getting a lot of vague or rambling answers to your questions, make sure it's not your fault. You may not be asking the question as crisply as you could. Be clear in your own mind what you need to know and why.

There are limits to brevity
There's an important caveat to seeking short answers. They can

prevent people from saying what they truly think (see candor below), or they can keep the other person from truly engaging their thinking to the analytic or creative level. If you strive too hard for brevity, you may miss important information that could improve outcomes or relationships. Or, you might damage the relationship by giving the other person the impression that they are wasting your time.

Questions to promote clarity
Recall that the three elements of lean communication that promote clarity are transparent logic, candor and directness, and user-friendly language. You can employ questions to encourage all three.

Structure
Most people, unless they've had special training, are not as orderly in their thinking—and hence their expression—as they could be. Their description of the issue or exposition of the problem could be circuitous or rambling, and contain unnecessary detail.

To help the other person discover/impose a structure if they're rambling, it's useful to have standard structures in your own mind, so you can ask the questions in order. For example, the problem/ solution structure:
- What's the problem?
- Why is it important to solve?
- What are the causes?
- What are the criteria for a solution?
- What alternatives have you considered?
- Which do you recommend and why?
- How will it be implemented?

Candor and directness
"If you do not seek dissent, it might seek you out anyway."
Jerry Fadem, The Art of Asking

We rely on the candor of others to ensure we're getting the information we need to make good decisions, but, as we saw in Chapter 6, others may be reluctant to tell us precisely what's on their minds. They may fear our reaction to what they say or want to spare our feelings. They may keep quiet out of a sense of futility (assuming it won't do any good to speak up), or simply because they assume we already know.

For all these reasons, we often need to actively seek out dissent, even if we would prefer to avoid it.

But some questions are better than others. For example, you could ask:

- Are you OK with the plan?

You may get a candid answer to this yes/no question. On the other hand, the other person may be afraid to voice their doubts, or they may infer that you are demanding agreement, not asking their opinion. So, how can we improve on that question?

- How comfortable are you with the plan?

Or, even better:

- What am I missing?
- What can we do to improve on it?

If the lack of candor stems from fear, your questions can encourage others to open up by showing vulnerability or ignorance on your part. Older readers will remember Columbo, the TV detective who disarmed suspects by asking a lot of innocent sounding questions. The guilty party felt safe in opening up to the naïve and bumbling questioner.

User-friendly language
Questions are a useful scalpel to cut through the FOG, either yours or theirs. Despite your own best effort to dispel FOG from your

communication, the listener may get confused, so your questions can check whether they got your meaning. More likely, they will use FOG in their communication with you, so you can ask questions to make them more specific or concrete.

Clarification questions are used to get better precision around two things: the noun or the adjective—in other words, quality and quantity. For example, if someone says, "we can soon have a significant impact on customer satisfaction".

- Can you quantify what you mean by "significant" amount?
- What do you mean by customer satisfaction? Do you mean survey ratings, or repeat purchasing?
- What specific "impact" are you predicting?
- Can you give me an example?
- What does "soon" mean?

How to ask questions

Even though every one of us has been asking questions ever since we could talk, there is actually a skill to it that we can improve. Some questions are definitely better than others. We'll first discuss which types of questions you should avoid, then examine the benefits of preparation, choosing between open and closed questions, and what to do before and after asking the question.

The wrong questions can create waste

You know the old saying that there's no such thing as a stupid question? It's not exactly true, although I would like to modify the language somewhat. I would say that there is definitely such a thing as a wasteful question—one that creates waste. A wasteful question is one that subtracts value, or makes it harder and longer to get to value in the conversation.

Wasteful questions can shut down candor and diverse thinking, even when the speaker means well. For example, it might seem that a questions such as "Does everyone agree?" might get dissenters to open up, but it can actually get them to shut down, because if no one speaks up at first, they may be reluctant to be seen as challenging the group consensus. There's another one that I'm embarrassed to admit I have used a lot in the past: "Does that make sense?" It's hard for someone to say no, because the question appears to contain the answer you're looking for, especially when you are higher ranking than the person being asked.

Questions can create distrust if they seem too one-sided. One-sided questions are those where it seems like you are pumping them for information that may help you, but they see no advantage to them in answering. Leading questions are also a form of this, because they might give the impression that you only care for one right answer.

They may create distrust if they are seen as trying to find fault, catch errors or build yourself up at their expense.

- Why did you do that?
- What were you thinking?
- What are you doing?

Do these pass the test?
- Negative questions: "Why didn't you think of that?" "Don't you care about doing a good job?"
- Leading questions: "Do you want to help the team?"
- Loaded questions: "Are you stupid or just sloppy?"
- Multiple questions: Are we going to ship on time? Why not? What have you been doing all this time?"
- Statements masquerading as questions: "Don't you think this is the most brilliant idea?"

Finally, it can pay to be economical in your use of questions, even when a lot of things may be unclear to you. If you ask too many, you can break up the flow of the conversation, or make it feel like a cross-examination.

Prepare your questions in advance

Most people think they can go with the flow and think of the appropriate questions to ask during the conversation, but that can be a big mistake. Even if you're reasonably skilled at it, you can always do better with a little preparation. Those who ask questions for a living, such as journalists, prepare carefully for the questions they ask. Professional salespeople have lists of questions that help them ensure they don't miss anything and that they cover the areas that must be covered to help the buyer reach the desired conclusion.

Preparing your questions ahead of time will also enable you to craft them properly and avoid inadvertently sending the wrong signals.

The lean idea of standard work, which is covered in Chapter 4, applies to questions as well and can actually save you a lot of time in your preparation. If you ask the same types of questions for each type of conversation (e.g. problem-solving discussion), you can quickly spot what information is missing from someone else's presentation of the situation.[5]

Closed or open?

There is a widespread misconception that one should always ask open-ended questions, but this is not always true. Closed-ended questions are better for some uses.

Closed questions are easy to answer; this can be good or bad, depending on your purpose.
- They help you to efficiently gather facts
- They're useful for locking in commitments
- They can be used to limit the scope of the conversation and promote brevity

Open questions can draw out feelings and ideas.
- They can encourage additional information, beyond what you're looking for.

- They can promote self-discovery in the listeners
- They stimulate thinking
- They allow for the unexpected
- They can project outside-in thinking and curiosity

What to do before and after you ask the question

It's efficient to ask your questions as directly as possible, but the briefest way may not be the leanest way. Sometimes it helps to add a preamble, which can provide context and show respect at the same time. From the other person's perspective, the best questions are those that they recognize will add value to them, not just to you, and providing context can help them see why the question is important.

Context can also improve the quality of answer you receive. If they don't know why you're asking, they can get defensive and avoid answering candidly. If they know why you're asking, they can prepare more appropriate answers to help you get there. (Some of this may already be done for you if you're having a lean conversation, and the other person knows the answer to the question.)

After asking your question, the smartest thing you can do is simply to shut up. Allow time for them to answer, which may sound obvious to you, but can be very rare in practice. For one thing, any silence longer than about one second can feel uncomfortable, both to the questioner and to the respondent. But waiting is critical. First, it shows respect for the other person because it demonstrates that you truly care to hear their answer. If you don't wait to hear their answer, they may infer that the answer is not that important to you. Second, it can yield better answers.

There's an idea in education called wait time, which simply means allowing time for the other person to answer the question.

Science educator Mary Budd Rowe conducted a study of wait time in classrooms and found that increasing the wait time from one second to three seconds boosted the length of the average answer from 7 words to 28. By giving the responder more time, it allowed them to process the question more deeply and thus improve their answer.[6] Researchers said that this extra time is needed to get people's participation and cognition; in effect, wait time shows preemptive respect for their answer.

Wait time applies twice, immediately after you asked the question, and then immediately after they answer. If you don't reply immediately after their initial answer, two things can happen. They may add to their answer, and often what is said second is the most important part. It also validates them by showing that you are thinking about what they said.

Wait time is simple but can be difficult. Silence is uncomfortable, and an insecure questioner will often re-word the question, or—even worse—answer it themselves. Resist the temptation and the length and quality of the responses you get will surely rise.

There are other ways besides direct questions to improve the flow of conversation between participants, and those are covered in the next chapter, on lean listening.

10

Lean Communication Key #10: Lean Listening

Call to Action
Use lean listening to improve your attention, interpretation, and responsiveness.

Summary
Listening is the most powerful tool we have for ensuring value and rooting out waste in communication. It's the best way to learn about what your listener values and to ensure they get it. For many of us, listening is even harder than speaking and contains at least as much waste. The solution is to harness the second conversation in your head to put AIR into your listening, by improving your Attention, Interpretation, and Response.

Everything we have covered so far in this book has been about the transmission side of the lean communication process, but reception is just as important. Since the first priority of lean communication is to create value as defined by the other person, you must listen to understand how the other person defines value and how they receive the message you transmit.

In addition, we saw in Chapter 8 how the pull system can help you deliver what the audience needs when they need it. The best tool you have for ensuring the pull system works is listening—specifically lean listening. Remember kanban signals from Chapter 8? They are essential to making the pull system work, but only if you receive, interpret and properly respond to the signals your "customer" sends in the form of questions and non-verbal indicators they display while you talk. They will tell you how your message is being received and alert you if you need to repeat, rephrase, clarify, or shift direction entirely.

We also need to focus on listening because there is at least as much potential waste in listening as there is in speaking. In general, we listen more than we talk; one study estimated that listening takes up 45% of our communication bandwidth. Other sources put it as high as 60%.[1]

Listening is a crucial skill for lean communication because it helps us:

- Understand the person we are speaking to
- Make adjustments to our message to ensure that we add value
- Gauge "customer satisfaction" with the "product" we deliver
- Reduce waste by improving our chances of getting things right the first time and reducing rework
- Ensure clarity and verify that the other person is receiving the message as we intend
- Draw out the other person's true intentions and meaning
- Help the other person be lean in *their* communication
- Respect the relationship

Before reading on, pause for a second to consider this question: in a dialogue, what percentage of your time should be spent listening?

Chances are, your answer was lower than mine. It's a trick question. You should spend *100%* of your dialogue time listening. That's because you should be listening even *while you're talking*. Don't get so engrossed in the process of transmission that you fail to see if and how reception is taking place.

Magic Leap CEO Peggy Johnson expressed this tendency in telecommunication terms when she told me that she is constantly frustrated by people who operate only on "half-duplex" mode—meaning they don't transmit and receive at the same time—and usually the transmit function is used much more than the receive![2]

This is especially helpful when you think that others may intentionally try to mask their reactions to what you're saying: maybe they don't understand but don't want to feel dumb, or they may not agree but don't want to seem difficult, and so on.

Most people are pretty good at suppressing their expressions when they want to, except for those immediate but ever-so-brief flashes called micro-expressions that are almost impossible to control. You won't catch them unless you are fully paying attention—even as the words are coming out of your own mouth.

It takes a lot of practice to become adept at catching and interpreting these nonverbal signals, and it's beyond the scope of this book, but it's a tremendously useful skill to cultivate.

It all starts with paying attention.

You're probably not as good a listener as you think you are
In my classes, most people freely admit that they are not always as good at listening as they could be, but most also think they can be excellent listeners when they consciously apply themselves to it. While it's true that you can step up your listening effectiveness in short bursts by making the effort, sometimes effort is not enough, as I demonstrate with a simple test. I tell them that I am going to

give them a set of instructions and then test them at the end to see how well they did at listening. They're allowed to take notes or do whatever they think will help.

Follow along and see how well you do, even though it should be easy for you since you're reading the instructions and not listening to them:

"You're the driver of the main street bus. At the first stop, three blue-eyed people get on the bus. At the second stop, four brown-eyed people get on, and one blue-eyed person gets off. At the third stop, two green-eyed people get on, and two people get off the bus.

Question: What color are the eyes of the bus driver?"

When I pose this test, about 10-20 percent of the participants answer it correctly. (Without going back and re-reading, do you know the answer?)[3]

Why do so few people get the right answer even though it's clearly laid out for them? I can't be sure, but I think it's because they are so focused on listening for what they think they will be tested on, that they ignore what they perceive to be unimportant. They heard "you're the driver" but they didn't listen to it, because they were eager to hear the hard facts they thought were going to be critical. This selective attention is what allows magicians to perform their feats and pickpockets to make a living.[4]

As this small demonstration shows, it's not enough just to try hard and focus on what the other person is saying. You need the right kind of focus. It's like driving a car: most of your attention is on the road directly ahead of you, but your peripheral vision also has to be alert to pick up threats from the side, such as a distracted driver straying into your lane. In listening terms, you need to find the right balance between listening *for* information and listening *to* the other person.

Hearing is not the same as listening

A moment's reflection on many of your daily conversations will show that mere hearing is a long way from actual listening.

Hearing is the physical act of registering the sounds that are coming out of someone's mouth; listening is the mental act of extracting both cognitive and emotional meanings from those sounds, and responding appropriately. Hearing is passive, listening is very active—which means it involves a lot of transmitting as well as receiving. Hearing is easy; in fact, it can be hard *not* to hear even when we try to. Listening, on the other hand, is hard work.

What is lean listening?

If you've read a book or taken a course on listening, you learned that the highest form of listening is empathic listening, where you show sensitivity and strong concern for what the other person is feeling. That is a useful and even virtuous skill to use for many of life's circumstances—but it is not the same as lean listening.

Lean listening is listening for the specific purpose of supporting and enhancing lean communication: ensuring that value is received as intended, with minimum time and effort on the part of both parties. Because the primary focus of lean is value, lean listening is less people-oriented and more action-oriented.[5] That's not to discount the importance of relationships, but it's a reminder of the primacy of outcomes.

Before we turn to specific lean listening techniques, let's stress three principles that will make you a better lean listener: collaboration, respect, and responsibility.

Lean listening is *collaborative*, because it's about co-creating value. Because two minds are better than one, it means being open to opportunities to elicit ideas from the other person that could make your idea and its application to the current situation even better and more useful. Fortunately, simply by listening carefully, you may encourage the other person to open up more and become more of a willing participant in the shared goal.

Lean listening is *respectful.* One of the tenets of lean thinking in general is respect for the individual, and what better way to show that, than by listening? Respect the fact that the other person brings value: approach every conversation as an opportunity to improve the situation or learn something, and your listening effectiveness, as well as your relationships, can't help but improve.

Lean listening is about *responsibility*. Apply the 51+ rule: whether you are speaking or listening, you should take at least 51% of the responsibility to ensure that the message is fully understood. Don't assume that just because you said it, the other person understood it as you intended; don't assume that just because you heard it, you understood it as they intended. This means that if you are the one presenting the idea, you need to pay close attention to how the idea is being received, and whether you are getting active commitment rather than passive acquiescence; if you're unsure, don't hold back from asking questions to ensure the level of agreement you're getting. If you're the listener, listen for <u>the question</u>: what do you want me to do and why?

Ten sources of listening waste

Listening seems so simple on the surface, but when you examine all the ways it can go wrong, it's actually a wonder that we can do it at all. There are at least ten sources of waste that can creep into the simple act of capturing value from what another person is saying.

Forming the message: What goes on in the speaker's mind is not what comes out of their mouth	
1. Speakers do not always say exactly what they are thinking	Speakers may hedge their meaning or delay getting to the point because they're concerned about your reaction or how they come across.
2. Words are imprecise carriers of meaning	The speaker may not choose the precise words to describe what they mean; the words they do choose may carry a different meaning to the listener.

Delivering: What comes out of the speaker's mouth is not always heard as intended	
3. Mismatch between non-verbal behavior and logical content	Because speakers don't always say what they're thinking or feeling, the content of their words may not match their expressions, tone of voice, or movements.
4. Our personal filters may limit or distort what we hear	Our own judgments and biases, cultural leanings, knowledge levels, values and attitudes will color what we hear and how we hear it.
5. We are easily distracted by things around us and thoughts in our head	Even when we try to concentrate on what's being said, our restless minds are constantly on alert for novelty and stimulus.
Hearing: What is heard is not always interpreted as the speaker intended	
7. Intention	We listen for what we want to hear, and may miss the rest; we form judgments which color how we interpret everything said after that; we listen only to argue or refute.
8. Working memory limitations	When the information or explanation comes faster than we can make sense of it, we can easily lose the thread of the dialogue.
Responding: Our response affects what the speaker will say next	
9. Feedback	While they're talking, we may be consciously or unconsciously sending them signals that will influence what they say.
Remembering: Retaining what we hear	
10. We forget a substantial part of what was said by the time we need to act on the information.	After a 10-minute oral presentation, most of us have already forgotten at least half of what we heard.

Put AIR into your lean listening

It's fortunate that, despite these ten sources of waste that impair effective listening, we can still manage to communicate fairly well.

That said, there are many opportunities for removing waste in communication through lean listening. We will look at three skill sets that will put AIR into your lean listening:

- Attention
- Interpretation
- Response

Attention

Let's go back to our lean production metaphor for a moment: if half the product your customer shipped to you fell off the truck between their loading dock and yours, that would be incredibly wasteful, wouldn't it?

In effect, the same thing happens when our attention wavers for just a moment and we miss some of the words being uttered. Our communication partners are not the only ones who suffer from attention deficit; we suffer from it just as much as they do.

Cranking our attention gauge from partial to full is not simply *paying* attention, because that word emphasizes the cost. I prefer the term *investing* attention because it rightly implies a payoff.

By investing attention, you will ensure not only that you receive the entire message, you will also get the added benefit that it encourages even more openness from the speaker, and you can create a virtuous circle that draws both of you into a much deeper and more meaningful conversation.

There are two routes to improve your attention: mental preparation before the communication and physical involvement during it.

Preparation
- If you are expecting to talk to someone about a particular subject it will help to become familiar with the topic, even if it is to refresh your memory.
- Think about what you would like to get from the conversa-

tion. Think about or jot down some questions ahead of time to prime your mind.

- Suspend your ego. Remind yourself to respect the speaker; know that you can profit or learn from anyone at any time.
- If someone else initiates the conversation, become interested in the topic. Ask yourself, "What can I learn or get from this conversation?"
- Resist the temptation to multitask, by removing distractors such as open computer screens. If you're talking with someone face to face, you may remove barriers, such as a desk between you and the speaker, or reduce distractions by setting aside what you are working on, closing the door, etc.

Physical Involvement

Becoming physically involved will greatly improve your communication effectiveness. Besides the obvious benefit of encouraging your counterpart to open up, it actually primes your own mind for more effective listening.

- Maintain effective eye contact
- Use head nods, smiles and facial expressions to show interest
- Face the other person squarely
- Keep an open position
- Lean slightly towards the person
- Take notes (sparingly)

These suggestions are simply common sense. We all know what to do, but we often need to remind ourselves to be mindful of the physical message we send while we listen. The person speaking to us definitely is!

Plan to Report

Plan to Report is one of the most powerful quick listening hacks you can use to maintain attention and help you organize what you're hearing. Imagine your boss had asked you to report back what was said in the conversation or presentation you just heard. Would that change the way you listened? You bet it would! If you use some of your extra processing capacity to rehearse in your mind how you will report this conversation, it's amazing how it automatically helps you keep your focus and listen for value, structure the logic, and strip out the inessential details.

Interpretation

Attention will ensure that you capture the other person's words and signals, but you still have to do something with them once you've caught them. You need to properly interpret the message, a task that is complicated by what's going on in your mind as you listen. In plain terms, you think much faster than the other person speaks, which can help you or hurt you.

In chapter 8, I introduced that nagging second conversation in your head that speaks up every time you have excess bandwidth. If you've ever tried to speak with someone on the phone while someone else is talking to you, you know how difficult it can be—and just because it's in your head doesn't make it any easier.

So, what can you do about it? The trick is not to try to silence your second conversation—you can no more slow down your rate of thinking than you can control your heartbeat. The trick is to *use* the second conversation to support your listening rather than interfere with it. The second conversation becomes a help and not a hindrance when it gets you to focus tightly on the value of what is being said, to find or impose order on it, and cut through the clutter of waste in their conversation.

Think of the second conversation as a coach who is in the room while you are talking to the other person, who is closely paying attention and is asking questions to make sense of what's being said and not said. But not just any random thought that comes to mind: this coach is *listening for lean* communication from the other party.

Think about it this way: if the other person is communicating in a perfectly lean manner, you would not have to improve your listening, because you would get exactly the information you need for your purposes as you need it. But since that usually doesn't happen, the main purpose of lean listening is to *help the other person be lean*. You do this by listening for the aspects of lean communication that contribute to value and waste, and ask questions or adjust where there are gaps.

The important thing about the second conversation is to keep it focused on asking questions only about what is being said or signaled in the moment, not about what you are planning to say in response. In effect, it's about being fully present, in both the spatial and cognitive meanings of that word.

The questions you ask yourself are the ones that keep you focused on finding the five major elements of lean communication by listening for value and for waste.

Listen for Value
You listen for value by listening for the key point and by being alert to the speaker's needs, whether expressed or implied.

Listen for the point
If your conversation partner is practicing lean communication, they will lead with their main point. If not, it's up to you to distill out their main point as quickly as possible, because it's the master key that makes everything else fall into place. Without it, it's hard to distinguish the relevant from the irrelevant, or the important from the merely interesting. Remember the "plan to report" listening hack? Ask yourself what the headline would be on that report you write. Ask yourself if you've heard the point, and if the answer is no, ask.

By listening for the main point, you may be doing the speaker's work for them. Nothing wrong with that: you may recall that one of the ways to add value is to reduce the other person's effort.

Take responsibility for ensuring the main point gets across, so they don't have to.

Listen for needs

Most of us are already pretty good at listening for needs in conversations—as long as it's *our* needs. But in productive business conversations, there are usually two other parties that could potentially benefit: the other person, and the larger purpose or enterprise.

Sometimes you have to do the work of finding needs because the person you're talking to does not always know what is best for them or for the larger purpose. So, besides listening carefully for their view of value, you must always be on the alert for signals that indicate additional implicit needs.

In conversation, these signals fall into two categories: intentions and obstacles. Intentions are where they want to go, such as their plans, goals, desired future states, and values. Obstacles are elements of the situation that hinder their realization of intentions, and they fall under four general categories as described in Chapter 1: Problems, Opportunities, Changes, and Risks (POCR).

Your counterparts may not be explicit in these, or even be totally aware of them themselves, so you must listen carefully for them; it's amazing how much extra you can pick up if you're alert for these. I once videotaped a sales roleplay in which the "buyer" revealed five potential intentions or obstacles in about thirty seconds. When we reviewed the tape, the seller had missed all five, and the buyer was not even aware of three of them that had come out of her own mouth! But what's interesting is that when we reviewed the video and looked specifically for signals of need, they popped right out.

Listening closely for needs is the best way to improve outcomes for all parties concerned; and you will definitely respect the relationship at the same time.

Listen for Waste

Part of doing the work for the other party is sifting out what's relevant, seeing their logical structure clearly, and deciphering their language.

Listen for relevancy

Apply the Four-I test when you listen: concentrate on identifying the integral and important information, enjoy the interesting without getting too distracted by it, and ignore the irrelevant. Mentally ask "So What?" periodically to ensure that what you are hearing contributes to the purpose of the conversation. If it doesn't, you are perfectly within your rights to ask the question out loud (as tactfully as you think you need to), to ensure that the content of the message is aligned with the purpose.

Listen for transparent logic

If the other person is communicating lean, following their logic should not be a problem, but if you can't spot an underlying pattern, you can help the other person communicate more clearly to you by asking them for the structure that you prefer. For example, most business proposals fall into either a problem/solution structure or an investment opportunity (and they're not mutually exclusive). If you can identify which of these applies, you can deploy your own mental template to help slot the incoming information in its proper place.

Listen to language

There is so much room for misunderstanding the language used even in ordinary conversation, but we often don't ask for clarification because we think it might make us look slow or ignorant. Don't let your ego get in the way of effectiveness; make it a practice of asking for clarification or definition, or perhaps a concrete example of an abstract term. If you can't picture it, you may not understand it—and often they may not either. For example, if someone says they want to improve quality, ask them to describe the specific gap between what is and what should be, using examples if possible. Listen especially for weasel words, which may indicate you need to dig a bit deeper to see if the speaker actually has data to back up his or her claims.

Response

You can listen perfectly attentively and grasp the speaker's exact meaning, and it still won't be enough; the "transaction" is only complete when the other person knows they have been heard. The best way to do this is to play back something they said, along with your reaction to what you heard. Let's look at three simple reflecting techniques and one responding technique:

Reflecting

Reflective listening describes verbal feedback you give to the speaker to demonstrate that you understand the content and/or feeling in their message and to give them an opportunity to correct or clarify if necessary.

Paraphrasing

This is simply feeding back to the speaker, in your own words, what you have heard. Paraphrasing lets the other speaker hear how their own message was received, which affords them an opportunity to confirm or correct your understanding.

To paraphrase effectively:
- Be concise—make your paraphrase shorter than the statement
- Rephrase key points only, not details
- Focus just on content
- Use your own words

"You think the deadline is too tight."

Reflecting feeling (active listening)
Reflecting feeling is a form of paraphrasing that lets the other person know that you are sensitive to what he or she is feeling. It takes skill to listen beyond the words for the underlying emotions, and then express empathy for what the customer is feeling.

- Focus on feeling words
- Reflect feelings back tentatively—don't come across as presumptuous
- Give them an opportunity to correct your perception
- Use this formula: "You feel _____ because _____."

"You're concerned, because you think we may miss the deadline."

Summarizing
Periodically, you can summarize what the other person has said. This demonstrates your overall understanding of the message and helps focus on key points. Once again, as in paraphrasing, a well-crafted summary can be one of your best listening tools.

Responding
From a relationship perspective, the most important task of listening is to make the other person feel that what they say matters to you.

That's why, while reflecting skills are useful, they may not be not enough. For example, have you ever had a conversation with a help desk when you have a complaint? You'll notice that they are well trained to use these reflecting skills of paraphrasing, active listening and summarizing. But if that's *all* they do, they may actually make you angrier, because while they are showing they understand, you don't really believe them unless they do something about it. That's where *responding* comes in.

For truly effective listening it's not enough just to show the other person you've heard. You have to take the next step and show them *you're doing something with what you heard*. Just as empathy is more than knowing what the other person is thinking and feeling—it's responding appropriately. Responding is the SO WHAT of lean listening.

"Your concern over late deliveries tells me we need to come up with a plan to eliminate the risk. Here's what we're going to do..."

E

Extras

If you stop reading now, you have the ideas to master lean communication and become a more valuable communicator as an individual contributor. But just knowing how does not mean that lean communication will necessarily come easy to you. You still have to practice and work consistently to improve your skills and embed productive lean communication habits into your daily work.

In addition, one of the likely side effects of becoming more valuable is that you are likely to rise to positions of leadership in your organization. Leadership communication poses its own challenges and opportunities above and beyond individual communication, so you may need the next chapter sooner than you think.

11

Lean Communication
for Leaders

Call to Action

As you rise in the organization, you must intensify your practice of lean communication, while making adjustments for power differences.

Summary

When you become a leader, lean communication becomes more important than ever, even as it poses its own special challenges and opportunities. You need to be aware of three special communication challenges that leaders face, so that you can adapt your approach to continue to focus on value, brevity, clarity and dialogue.

Caution: becoming a better communicator may accelerate your rise in your organization. But that does not mean you can relax. When you rise to a position of leadership, lean communication becomes more important than ever, but it also may become more difficult.

First, you will communicate more than ever before. According to one study, leaders spend 80-85% of their time communicating[1], and I suspect that a good part of the remaining 15% is spent thinking about what to say and how to say it.

Second, your position magnifies your power to produce both

value *and* waste. Therefore you have a corresponding obligation to do it more effectively and efficiently than ever before—to pay even more attention to lean communication.

The general purpose of your communication as a leader is still the same: to get things done through others by communicating useful information that they can use to drive effective action and valuable outcomes. As Steve Dakolios, CEO of Federal Packaging told me: a leader's job is to convert potential energy into kinetic energy.[2] Your communication crucially affects both the measure and direction of that energy.

The same ten keys of lean communication apply to leadership communication as they do to any ordinary form of business communication, but there are some differences, and that's the subject of this chapter.

But before going straight to value, waste and dialogue, it's important to address a serious potential condition that may affect your leadership communication as you climb the slopes of leadership: I call it "altitude sickness."

Altitude sickness and leadership

Altitude sickness can strike any leader, and it affects the quality, style and content of your communication in three ways:
- Ethos Illusion
- Empathy Erosion
- Control Paradox

Ethos Illusion

The simplest way to describe the ethos illusion is that it's easy to become lazy. That's because as you gain in authority, communication seems to get easier: people are more likely to listen carefully while you speak, laugh at your jokes, ask your advice, and do what you suggest. The danger is that you may stop working so hard on your lean communication skills.

Think about things that once came easy to you, that you'd be hard-pressed to do well now: maybe remembering phone numbers; doing mental math; driving a stick shift. As we find newer and easier ways of achieving our goals, of course it makes sense to stop using the old skills, and it doesn't cause any harm—until we need them.

Stanford Business School professor Jeffrey Pfeffer recently wrote:

"A colleague of mine who teaches at Duke University recently told me about a speech he attended on campus by the CEO of a company that is best left unnamed here. It turned out to be a terrible speech — riddled with platitudes, internal inconsistencies, and false facts. On his way out the door, my friend overheard two students discussing what they'd just heard.

"He's incredibly rich," one of them said. "He must be smart."

That CEO gave a terrible speech, but paid no price for it. Do you think he's going to work hard for his next one? Rich people, famous people, people with impressive titles: they all get a pass."[3]

I call it the ethos illusion after Aristotle's three modes of persuasion: *logos* (logic), *pathos* (emotion) and *ethos*, (character and personal credibility). Aristotle told us that ethos is the most important, which makes sense because listeners are also lazy; it's easier to take a mental shortcut—relying on who the speaker is, and unfortunately that comes to mean the speaker's title or authority—than it is to listen carefully, make sense of data, and carefully weigh arguments.

When credibility isn't automatic for you, you work harder: you gather data, think carefully about your logic, and present it in terms of what the listeners will care about most. In short, you prepare. But preparation takes time and effort, and if you're a leader with a lot more important issues on your plate, surely it's lean to save either one if you can?

When "because I said so" gets the compliance you want, why

rely on logos? Why make the effort to carefully prepare your case, to anticipate objections, to polish your prose, to weigh your words before you speak?

The result is that unintentionally and imperceptibly, the quality of your thinking and your expression may suffer.

Empathy Erosion

You can avoid the ethos illusion as long as you care about what your followers think.

But, what if you stop caring about what others think? What if you start seeing others more as tools to exploit to get your way? It's called *empathy erosion*, and unfortunately it's a condition that is also likely to become worse the higher you go.

Leaders should be able to effortlessly take others' perspective— it should actually be *easier* for you as a leader, because after all you've been in their shoes but they haven't been in yours.

But what happens in reality to perspective taking as you gain power? Unfortunately, a lot of evidence suggests that you're less likely to take others' perspectives into account as you become (or at least think you become) more important. UC Berkeley professor Dacher Keltner says, "When we experience absolute power, our attention shifts to our own interests and desires, thus diminishing our capacity for empathy—understanding what others feel and think."[4]

Columbia Business School professor Adam Galinsky has demonstrated that people who are primed to feel powerful even for just a short time, show diminished empathy in three ways.

- It makes them more likely to see things from their own perspective, not that of others.
- It's harder to imagine that others don't know what they do, and they are more likely to get impatient when others don't get it.
- They become less accurate at reading others' emotions.

Galinsky summarizes by saying: "...power was associated with a reduced tendency to comprehend how others people see, think, and feel."[5]

To make it even worse, power makes you view others more instrumentally; you see them less as a person and more as a tool that you can exploit to achieve your own goals.

Empathy erosion can even be measured. There is a phenomenon called motor resonance, which simply means that when we observe someone else doing an activity, the same areas that are firing in their brains during the activity are firing in ours. We *feel* them, and it's what helps us imagine things from their perspective. But those with more power showed diminished motor resonance in MRI scans of their brains. They actually do think differently! As social psychologist Heidi Grant Halvorson says: "It's not so much that they think they are better than you as it is that they simply do not think about you at all."[6]

Why does empathy erosion matter?

If you step back and look at the problem practically and non-judgmentally, is it really such a bad thing if leaders are less empathetic? After all, there are times when the job demands less empathy; sometimes you have to make hard decisions for the greater good and if you tore yourself up about each person it's going to affect, it would probably paralyze you.

And you have so many important tasks on your plate that it's tempting to put efficiency and speed over relationships. You just don't have the time, and if you don't get it done, they'll find someone who can.

But there's the paradox: the fact that you don't have enough time to devote to thinking about the people side is exactly why you need to take the time to think about the people side: no one—not even you—can do everything by themselves. You have to trust others to do things, and you need for them to give their best efforts.

Who will give their best efforts for someone they don't think cares about them?

Coercion gets you only so far. As Dwight Eisenhower said, "Leadership is the art of getting someone else to do something you want done because he wants to do it." So, think of empathy as an investment in long-term leadership effectiveness.

Control Paradox

As a leader, you value predictability. That's what plans are for, and what communication is meant to ensure. You plot your moves, forecast their results, and communicate them to the people who have to execute. When the task is simple, and you have a pretty good idea of what future conditions will be like, you can specify very clearly what you want people to do and expect that they're not going to encounter many exceptions. If they do, they can ask for direction and you'll have plenty of time to make the appropriate adjustments.

But when too many changes or unexpected events happen at once, that comfortable system can quickly break down, and there is much more room between intentions and results. When you say do X because you expect Y will happen—but instead Z happens, or Q or K or some totally unexpected such letter, you feel a loss of control. When the situation is slippery, your impulse is to tighten your grip; you put in tighter controls in the form of additional detail: "when this happens, do this."

More detail may help, but sometimes it's just clutter that overwhelms the person on the spot who is trying to figure out how to react to the novel situation. It may be an extreme example, but I'm reminded of the recent tragic picture of pilots rapidly thumbing through a loose-leaf manual as their 737 pitches up and down violently and seemingly randomly—and we all know how that scene ended.

Besides, tighter controls require more metrics, which means

more reporting, which means less work creating value, while at the same time sending a message to followers that you don't trust them to use their own judgment, which stifles initiative, which causes you to impose even tighter and more stringent controls. You become more internally focused, and more and more of the work you do does not contribute to value for the end customer.

The drive for control means well, because it's meant to prevent waste, but reducing or preventing waste, while extremely important, is never the main reason for doing anything; creating value for a customer is. But when reporting replaces dialogue as a means of communication; it makes you—not the end customer—the arbiter of what constitutes value, and thus violates the most important principle of lean.

Forewarned is forearmed. You must guard against the ethos illusion, empathy erosion and the control paradox. Now, let's turn our attention to positive ways to improve your lean communication as a leader.

How Leaders Deliver Value

Communication has value when it leads to one or more of the following:
- Improved business outcomes
- Improved personal outcomes
- Relationship is respected

So far, so good. But what's different about leadership communication?

Improved business outcomes

Your first responsibility as a leader is for improved business outcomes. By definition, the leader is responsible for something bigger than a single person—bigger than any single follower and certainly bigger than yourself. You are the spokesperson and cheerleader for the big picture. If you don't speak on behalf of the larger purpose and group goals, who will?

In lean terms, that means that you should explicitly explain the WIFU, or "What's In It for Us?". What's the business reason for what you're telling them? Don't assume they already know; don't assume they don't need to know; don't assume they don't care, because they do. And if they don't, it's your job to give them reasons to care.

Some leaders play things close to the vest, and tell subordinates only what they need to know to do their jobs. Maybe they buy into the old Frederick Taylor idea that: "You're not supposed to think. There are other people paid for thinking around here." Maybe it's because they've fallen into the ethos illusion, and think that "because I said so" is good enough reason. Maybe they think it's more efficient; because it saves time not having to explain their rationale.

But there are good reasons to share the big picture and provide the "why" in your communications. The control paradox reminds us that complex and dynamic environments present novel situations to front-line employees faster than the leader can react, so the person on the spot can benefit from having a clear idea of how their decisions may affect the larger enterprise.

Second, they also feel more connected to the purpose of the enterprise, so they are more likely to put in discretionary effort. It may make the difference between a front-line employee telling a customer it's not his job, versus taking the initiative to make sure the customer is happy.

Third, when they know what the big picture is supposed to look like, they may have other pieces of the puzzle that they are more likely to offer up if they know they're important. As Steve Jobs said, "It doesn't make sense to hire smart people and tell them what to do; we hire smart people so they can tell us what to do."

Improved personal outcomes

Even though WIFU takes precedence, you may still have to appeal to personal self-interest, or WIFM. This may seem unnecessary, because there is always at least an implication that they will do what you say if they know what's good for them.

But there are three levels of agreement: compliance, commitment, and leadership. Compliance means that they go along with your idea. They may say yes, or agree not to block your efforts. At the next level, they take an emotional and personal interest in the idea and commit to seeing that the idea gets implemented and become enthusiastically committed to it. This is the difference between following the letter of your request and promoting the spirit as well. At the highest level, they make the idea their own and take an active leadership role in promoting and extending it.

If simple compliance is all you're after, it would be wasteful to say anything more, but if you want more, you need to address their self-interest, both extrinsic and intrinsic.

It's easy to appeal to your listeners' extrinsic self-interest; you've got plenty of sticks and carrots at your disposal. But appealing only to extrinsic motivators can actually create more waste in the long-run, in the sense that you may be leaving a lot of effort, engagement, and creativity on the table if that's all you rely on.

As a leader it makes much more sense to tap into that engagement by appealing to intrinsic motivation. It's the difference between having followers who are "coin-operated" vs those who are self-motivated. It's the difference between transactional leadership and inspirational leadership. Leaders who inspire through their communication are about as lean as can be, because they create more value through motivating greater effort, and they greatly reduce the need to constantly keep communicating, checking and reminding people what they should be doing.

Focusing on personal outcomes is also a great way to combat empathy erosion. Research shows that when leaders are reminded that the goal requires them to see others' individual differences, they can actually do it more effectively than the less powerful; so maybe their empathy isn't eroding, it's simply being put aside for most of their tasks. The best reminder, of course, is to cultivate outside-in thinking until it becomes a habit.

Relationship is respected

Business and personal outcomes are about results, and relationships are about people. Leaders can benefit from the proper balance between the two. According to a survey of over 60,000 employees, leaders who were primarily results-focused were rated as "great" 14% of the time; people-focused leaders 12% of the time; leaders who focused equally on both, 72% of the time! If that sounds obvious to you, reflect on the estimate by David Rock that only 1% of all leaders do this.[7]

Relationships that are based on mutual trust and respect create value in two ways. First, everyone feels happier and more engaged, and second, because that translates into better business performance in general. A study by Gallup reported that companies in the top quartile of engagement are 21% more profitable and 17% more productive than companies in the bottom quartile.[8] (Of course, if you need studies to convince you to treat people well, you've probably already stopped reading by this point.)

Sharing information about the big picture and appealing to your followers' self-interest both show respect to your followers and enhance the relationship in and of themselves, but you can go even further if you strive to bring one or more of these three "social gifts" to every encounter:

Appreciation: Make people feel important. You can do this easily by simply paying attention to them, soliciting their input, praising them sincerely and specifically, and giving generous credit for success.

Connection: Connect with people on a personal level and find things you have in common. Some companies, such as Southwest Airlines, make this feeling of "family" a powerful part of their culture.

Elevation: Make people feel good. As Daniel Goleman reminds us: "Everyone watches the boss. People take their emotional cues from the top…even when leaders are not talking, they were watched more carefully than anyone in the group."[9] You have to take special care to project an upbeat, elevated attitude even when you don't feel like it—*especially* when you don't feel like it!

Brevity

In leadership communication, brevity is complicated. On the one hand, it's still a good idea not to take any more of your listeners' time than you need to get your message across. Being concise can also make you sound more confident and sure of your message, which is important for any leader.

There is one area, though, in which you can and should violate the principle of brevity, and that is repetition. It may seem wasteful to repeat a message that has already been heard; repetition is rework, which implies that the product was not made right the first time.

If you're asking for a decision or specific action, repetition *is* wasteful. But a lot of leadership communication is more general, such as communicating a vision or setting guidelines that people can follow over time, and that can't realistically be done in just one shot.

For example, let's assume you announce a new strategy that you want the whole company to follow. How many people, on first hearing the message, will enthusiastically commit to it right then and there and resolve to change how they work? Realistically, some won't hear, some won't understand, some won't take you seriously, some won't buy in, all will forget at least part of what you said. In this case, *not* repeating your strategy and your commitment to it is wasteful.

More is probably better, because it ensures that your message gets through, and it shows that you're serious. Any parent knows that saying something once is almost never effective. Value doesn't happen just because it's uttered; it has to be heard, understood, agreed and remembered.

That's why, for important ideas, Jack Welch says that a leader has to be relentless and boring. If you think you've said it enough times, you probably haven't. Conventional wisdom says it takes at least seven exposures to an advertising message before in sinks in, but that may just be a message told by the advertising industry to sell more ad time. One formal study done showed that persuasion increased up to three repetitions, and then began to decrease at five or more repetitions.[10]

One way to avoid diminishing returns is to inject a little variety. Repeat the same message but vary the way you say it, or substitute different stories and examples. Try using different channels—that will help keep it fresh for you and for your followers.

Clarity

Unlike brevity, the need for clarity is not that complicated. You may not always have to be brief, but you always have to be clear. For leadership communication, clarity is at least as important as adding value. That's because, as a leader, you create value through others, so your most important task is to give them the direction and motivation to act towards a common and worthwhile goal. You don't have all the answers, but by being clear about the big things such as vision, values, priorities and goals, you can enable, empower and encourage others to find the answers.

As Jeffrey Pfeffer says, "A leader's job is to reduce uncertainty, not create it."[11] Uncertainty is wasteful. Only about one-half of workers say they know what's expected of them at work.[12] Imagine how much waste there is when someone does not know where to apply themselves half the time.

Besides reducing waste and increasing effort, clarity can also expose disagreement with your message. This may sound wasteful, but it affords an opportunity to openly discuss differences and resolve them before they get out of hand. But that means that you have to pay close attention to LC Key #6: Candor and Directness.

Candor

Candor is fairly straightforward. In your own communication, you should strive to be as candid and transparent as possible, with one exception. If the situation is especially challenging, you should give your followers the respect of knowing they can handle the truth. But you are perfectly justified in hiding your own fears or lack of confidence. People don't always appreciate vulnerability from their leaders. When things were looking bleak for Britain after the fall of France in June 1940, Churchill stiffened the British spine with his famous "we shall fight on the beaches" speech. What people then didn't realize is that right after he finished the speech, he growled: "We shall hit them on the heads with broken bottles, because that's bloody well all we've got."

Candor works both ways; if you can dish it out, you have to be able to take it as well. That means you have to make it safe for others to speak up, even when it's bad news. Fierce Inc. surveyed 1,400 executives and employees and found that while 99% said they valued honesty and openness, 70% did not believe their own organization lived up to that ideal.[13] When people are afraid to speak their minds, problems get hidden, learning is suppressed, poor performance goes unchallenged, and mistrust breeds—all potential sources of waste.

Directness

Lean communication is biased toward directness, because direct speech is clear speech. Stating a point directly, in as few words as possible, is both efficient and clear, so it definitely reduces waste in communication. In general terms, you want to be as direct as possible, especially when speaking to groups.

But when it comes to coaching, there are two good reasons for dialing back direct speech. First, don't forget that that's a human being you're talking to, and human beings are prey to those pesky things called feelings, especially when their personal status is challenged. If they refuse to listen to your message because they feel slighted, or worse, determine to do the opposite, whatever you've gained in efficiency, you've more than thrown away in terms of effectiveness.

When giving feedback, of course you have to be clear. But there's a huge difference between clarity and "brutal honesty", which some leaders seem to brag about as a badge of toughness. Clarity is about identifying and effectively communicating the gap between actual and desired performance. Brutality is about being savage, cruel, or inhuman, according to the dictionary. Is this what you want to be when giving feedback to others?

Second, as a coach you often get better results from followers when they come up with their own ideas and plans for improvement. So, rather than directly telling them what to do, you indirectly guide them to the right conclusions by asking questions.

Dialogue

If you want to be a more effective leader, remove the megaphone from your mouth and hold it up to your ear.

Why do you need dialogue in leadership communication? When you know what has to be done, isn't it more efficient to just tell people what to do, and have them do it without bothering to question you?

The reality is that, despite how hard you work to produce brief, clear and valuable messages, you usually need dialogue to close the deal—to ensure that the message has had its intended effect and to make adjustments if not.

Dialogue can prevent or mitigate the three leadership traps you may fall into. You're less likely to rely on the ethos trap of "because I said so" when you welcome open questioning and disagreement. Empathy erosion is less likely when you're having meaningful conversations with individuals rather than a faceless mass of followers. Control becomes both lighter and more effective for two reasons: everyone understands each other better, and you get a clearer picture of what's happening outside your isolated corner office.

Dialogue can add value by producing better ideas, more vigorously executed. Better ideas result from productive disagreement and broader input from people with diverse viewpoints, experiences, and knowledge sets. Second, it gets people more engaged, and that makes them more productive.

Dialogue promotes clarity in both directions. Without it, you can't be sure people understand your intentions, and you have no idea how your intentions translate into real world results.

Finally, dialogue is an excellent antidote to the ethos illusion. You are less likely to fall back onto "Because I said so" when you open your mind and your ears to others' thinking.

Ways to improve dialogue

The simplest way to improve dialogue is to be accessible. Announce an open-door policy and mean it. But that's passive, and it's also reactive. It's tempting to rely on reports and what your immediate reports tell you, but that information can't help but be colored by filters and silos which may prevent you from getting a true picture.

So, regardless of how busy you think you are, you need to get out of your office and engage people at various levels. It's called MBWA, Management by Walking Around, and it does two things for you. It shows people you care. At the same time, by being random it prevents people preparing for your visit and showing you only what they want you to see, Potemkin village style.

A more structured form of MBWA is *going to the gemba*, literally, the "actual place" where the value creation happens, in front of customers, on the shop floor, and in the offices. Toyota Chairman Fujio Cho suggests, "Go see, ask why, show respect".

Formal meetings can be a good forum for dialogue, but keep them small—30-40 participants, tops—because people are reluctant to speak up in larger groups. But here's where the "show respect" part comes in: be prepared to be vulnerable, to admit that you may not have all the answers, and to accept criticism. And, if you recall lean listening, you have to close the loop by doing something about what you hear.

There's a formal process in lean called *hoshin kanri*, also called policy deployment, in which strategic plans are cascaded to the appropriate levels to ensure consistency and alignment. Using a process called "catchball", leaders toss ideas down a level, who then toss back their own input. Some version of *hoshin kanri* is an effective way to avoid the control paradox, because it improves the transfer of knowledge to and from the center, and frees up people to get valuable work done without constant monitoring and correction. When subordinates have to make a quick decision in a new situation, they ask themselves: *"What would my boss tell me to do if he knew what I know now?"*

How to get people to open up
One of the major challenges of leadership dialogue is to get people to open up and speak their minds to superiors. They have to feel safe, as discussed in Chapter 6.

But safety isn't enough, because people keep quiet for other reasons than fear of consequences. They may feel like it won't make a difference because no one will pay attention. They may be naturally loath to speak up to people they perceive as more powerful.

Even a well-meaning culture may discourage speaking out in certain circumstances. For example, a strong data-driven culture may generally be a good thing, but when it prevents people from voicing their doubts because they don't have hard data to back up their feelings, bad things may happen, as NASA discovered after both the Challenger and Columbia disasters.[14]

And then there's the old idea of "don't bring me a problem unless you have a solution." It's meant to tamp down griping, but it can also keep you from finding out about potential problems before they get out of hand. If someone sees a problem and doesn't know how to solve it, do you really want them to keep quiet about it until they've figured out a solution they can present to you?

So when things seem to be going fine, you may need to draw people out. One of the best examples I've heard comes from Alfred P. Sloan, former Chairman of GM, who once ended a senior executive meeting by saying: "Gentlemen, I take it we are all in complete agreement on the decision here. Then I propose we postpone further discussion of this matter until the next meeting to give ourselves time to develop disagreement, and perhaps gain some understanding of what the decision is all about."

Create a culture where people not only feel safe, but feel a responsibility to bring up bad news or disagreement. Lean factories have an *andon* cord, which any employee may—no, must—pull any time they see a problem. It's like the public service ads that say: "See something, say something".

Informality is a helpful way to get people to open up because it reduces power distance—people feel freer to speak up when they are not blatantly reminded of the rank difference. That's one reason that hierarchical structures such as Japanese companies and the Royal Navy encourage after hours karaoke and drinking, or dinners and outside team activities, respectively.

Informality doesn't mean you have to trash the chain of command, just that you have the right balance. Rex Geveden, who made several critical decisions as he rose to assistant administrator of NASA, put it this way: "The chain of communication has to be informal, completely different from the chain of command."[15]

Ask more questions. Drop the pretense that, as a leader, you have to have all the answers and all the good ideas. Questions engage and empower followers. Remember these wise words from Lao Tzu:

"A leader is best when people barely know he exists, when his work is done, his aim fulfilled, they will say: we did it ourselves."

Here are some additional tips to make you a better listening leader:
- Speak last. Let others express their opinions before they hear yours.
- When people do speak up, listen carefully and fully; don't rush to answer or solve their problem.
- Draw people out. Frequently, the first answer out of someone's mouth is not the best or the most candid, so invite them to say more. "Tell me more about that…" is a great phrase.
- Practice responsive listening. Show people they've been heard.

I need to close with one final reminder: *dialogue is <u>not</u> an abdication of leadership.* Just because you're listening to input does not mean that you have to accept it. It's not a popularity contest, or mindless consensus seeking. You still have the responsibility to make the hard decisions.

But you will make better decisions and get better results when you engage your followers in purposeful and productive dialogue. In short, you will be a better leader.

12

Sustaining and Growing Lean Communication Skills

Call to Action

Sustain and grow your skills by practicing the techniques of lean communication and improving in small ways consistently over time.

Summary

This book began with a call to action: that you should adopt the mindset and practices of lean communication. If you've made it this far, you have probably adopted the mindset already, and that's a great start. But take it from me, the practices don't come easy—that's why we call them practices. Fortunately, if you consistently follow a process to make small daily improvements, you will soon become a confident and effective lean communicator.

This is the shortest chapter, but it covers the longest phase of becoming a lean communicator.

The first step in becoming a Lean Communicator is to adopt the mindset. A mindset is defined as an attitude or intention, and having a Lean Communication mindset is a necessary first step that will concentrate your mind on delivering value. As you focus more on value, you will more clearly see waste, so you can work on rooting it out.

But even the best of intentions can be difficult to carry out until they become regular habits, and you will find that it's not easy at first. You will have to overcome ingrained habits of thought and behavior. For example, when someone asks you a question, it's easy to answer immediately, and deliver a long, rambling answer without first pausing to think.

Outside-in thinking and identifying waste both take time, attention and effort. In short, every one of the practices and skills outlined in this book requires work on your part until you can make them a natural and effortless part of everything you do.

However, the good news is that you will also find that it gets easier the more you do it. Don't try to change everything at once— that's a sure recipe for failure. Rather, focus every day on just one or two of the skills.

Think small

In 2003, David Brailsford took over as coach of the British national cycling team. In 76 years of Olympic competition, Britain had won one gold medal, and no British cyclist had ever won a Tour de France in 110 years of trying. They were so bad that one bicycle manufacturer had refused to sell bikes to them for fear that it would damage their image.[1]

Just five years later, the team won 60% of the available gold medals at the Beijing Olympics, and then topped that with nine Olympic records in the 2012 London games. They also won the Tour de France for the first time in that year, and have continued to dominate that race ever since.

To get such outstanding results, Brailsford must have come in and made immediate radical changes, right?

That was not the case at all. Brailsford decided to think small, reasoning that it would be too daunting for his team to contemplate the vast gulf between their current performance and an Olympic podium.

Instead, he focused on what he calls the "aggregation of marginal gains". Brailsford and his team reasoned that if they could get just 1% improvement out of each item, it would add up to major gains in time.

The team looked for ways to make small improvements to hundreds of tiny and seemingly unimportant factors, including:

- Teaching riders how to wash their hands to reduce sickness
- Painting the floor of the team truck white to spot dust that affected maintenance
- Testing different fabrics in wind tunnels to reduce drag
- Changing pillows and mattresses so that athletes would sleep in the same position every night

Brailsford got the idea from his MBA studies, where he learned about the lean concept of *kaizen*.

Kaizen: sustaining and growing your skills

If adopting the practices of lean communication were easy, it would not have been worth a whole book to describe them. As you've probably seen by now, it's not easy to change communication habits acquired over a lifetime. Hopefully it won't appear as daunting to you as winning an Olympic medal, but it can still seem to be a difficult goal. But don't despair. Through the magic of *kaizen*, you can make many small changes that over time can lead to a complete transformation in your skill and effectiveness.

The concept of kaizen is an idea from the Toyota Way that has worked its way into the general culture, so it probably does not need much explanation. However, remembering that assumptions can be dangerous, here's a concise definition and explanation.

The word kaizen comes from the Japanese characters "kai", meaning change, and "zen", meaning good. So, it means change for the better. It also includes the idea of continuous improvement, which means that you don't make a one-time change and then stop. Rather, you constantly look for ways to improve even on your improvements. As we've seen, it's so easy for waste to creep into our regular communication, that it should not be difficult to constantly refresh your sources of possible improvements!

Kaizen works mathematically not only because things add up, but because of the magic of compounding. A small percentage improvement continuously applied over time means that each successive improvement is larger than the last, and that can make a huge difference over time. Small quantitative changes eventually morph into qualitative change and growth.

But kaizen also works because of the way our minds work. While we're often exhorted to set big goals for ourselves, the size of the goals can sometimes be self-defeating. Big goals can stress us out; they engage our mind's self-defense mechanism and engender fear. How many times have you set yourself a big goal—say, a new year's resolution—and had it fail? Kaizen can help melt resistance because it allows for—indeed, encourages—small changes that are easy for our minds to assimilate.

Small changes are also easier to describe in concrete terms. "Become a better lean communicator" is too broad to envisage, but "When sending an email, write a headline in the subject line," creates a crisp picture. So what? Clarity motivates, and clarity illuminates the path.

Applying Kaizen

So, in the interest of clarity, what are some concrete and practical steps you can take to apply kaizen to your lean communication journey?

1. Select your highest priorities for immediate improvement.
2. Write down clear implementation intentions.
3. Review.
4. Repeat. Repeat. Repeat.

Select your highest priorities

By now, you've probably realized that there is communication waste everywhere you look, so it probably won't be too difficult to identify areas to work on. And if there are, just wait a page or two.

So you may find it helpful to identify and write down the first few specific items or areas you want to work on, and then select just one to start.

Some of these may have become immediately obvious to you as you've read through the book. Perhaps you recognized a wasteful communication practice and maybe felt a twinge of guilt. If you're not sure, start by self-monitoring: consciously pay attention to yourself as you engage in regular communication. You could even take it a step further by either asking others for feedback, or even videotape yourself.

Once you start noticing and/or brainstorming, you may find dozens of ways to make small improvements. You can begin anywhere within the keys of Adding Value, Brevity, Clarity and Dialogue.

There is a more complete list of small improvement opportunities in the appendix, and any one that you choose to work on can add value or reduce waste. But some areas may offer higher payoffs or more immediate improvements, so here is a suggested priority of ideas to get you started.

Lean listening

Although adding value is the first imperative of lean communication, I begin with listening because it is a great way to develop awareness of your own and others' behaviors and tendencies that either add value or generate waste. The first step to improving any skill is a clear-eyed assessment of your current level.

In lean terms, remember from Chapter 4 that Taiichi Ohno, said that eliminating waste is not the problem; spotting it, is. By working on your listening you will automatically start spotting so many more ways to take waste out of your own communication. Besides, simply by listening more effectively, you will find more ways to add value to those you talk to, and improve the relationship at the same time!

Small changes to become a better lean listener include:
- Remind yourself to listen for lean in at least one conversation a day.
- As your counterpart talks, try to extract their bottom line.
- Apply the *so what* test as you listen.
- Listen for their logical structure.
- Practice the "Plan to Report" hack.

Add value
If you're not adding value, it does not matter how brief or clear you are, so it pays to work on it next.

You must always strive to understand and frame your communication in terms of improving your listeners' outcomes while respecting the relationship.
- Create some sort of reminder or ritual to prime yourself to think outside-in at least once per day
- Write down your perception of your counterpart's needs before the next conversation or meeting. (Look for "POCR chips")
- Practice being clear about your ask at the start of the conversation

Brevity
- Practice BLUF
- Use headlines instead of subjects for emails
- When planning your arguments, ask so what at least three times

Clarity
- Signal your structure up front with verbal or written agendas
- Go through your presentations and identify smoke and FOG
- Pay attention to your own hedges and hesitations

Dialogue
- Practice the 4 + 2 Ps of answering questions
- Practice signaling your bullet points up front
- Prepare questions in advance for critical conversations

Implementation intentions

Once you've decided on your highest priorities, you then need to do something about the items you identify. It helps enormously to be very clear in your own mind exactly *how* you intend to work on the change you've targeted.

Remember implementation intentions from Chapter 7? This technique has been proven to be highly effective in reminding and motivating desired behaviors. Rather than vaguely saying you're going to try to get better, think about *specifically* what you will do differently and when. So, you might say, "When I go to the meeting on Tuesday, I will consciously try to start with the bottom line up front every time I'm asked a question." Implementation intentions work well if you only go through them in your mind, but they work even better if you write them down. You'll be amazed at how your mental reminder will kick in when you're in the actual situation you envisioned.[2]

Review

Periodic review of your progress is another great way to ensure that your mental reminders pop up when you need them, until the mental reminders stop because the practices have become automatic. Periodic review will help not only to gauge your progress and make adjustments, but also to keep the practice of lean communication salient in your mind.

After a while, you will catch yourself paying attention to how you're communicating and make adjustments. Each time you do so, it's like doing another repetition in an exercise—you will get stronger, and it will get easier.

You can also review your progress at set intervals, or conduct after-action reviews after important conversations, presentations, or meetings.

Repeat

When you feel confident enough in your improvement on the first skill, select another and apply the same process to it. Continue until satisfied. You don't need to improve much every day, as long as you keep it up.

For example, a 1% improvement does not seem like much, but what happens when it compounds? If you could improve 1% every day for a year, you would be 37x better at the end of the year. Or, if you could reduce waste by 1% a day during that time, you would all but eliminate it. It's not realistic to expect improvements every day so consistently, but it is clear that effort and patience can accomplish great things. And no, we're not talking about anywhere near 10,000 hours of deliberate practice to start noticing gratifying results!

It's also important to maintain perspective. You will have setbacks along the way, or stretches of time where you feel like you're not making any progress at all. But, just like a sledgehammer against concrete, nothing seems to happen until it all finally goes.

A little bit each day quickly adds up, and over time you will notice your communication will be more valuable, crisper, and more attuned to the value the customer needs. More importantly, your listeners will notice!

A Final Word

At the beginning of this book, I wrote that life as we know it would not be possible without effective communication. I wrote those words long before I'm writing these. As I write this final word, the world is going through the covid-19 crisis. If nothing else, it should remind us that all of us have an obligation to be part of the solution, not the problem. If every one of us makes a sincere effort to add value every time we communicate, the world can't help but become a better place.

Appendix

Kaizen Improvement Ideas

Add Value	
Make It about Them	<ul><li>Take stock of your talk-listen ratio</li><li>Think of WIFM/WIFU before conversation</li><li>List extrinsic and intrinsic needs</li><li>Try to anticipate POCRs they face</li><li>Practice bringing social gifts</li><li>Create a ritual to activate outside-in thinking</li></ul>
Answer the Question (ATQ)	<ul><li>Remind yourself what your purpose is before every planned conversation</li><li>Practice giving your ask up front</li><li>Narrow down and clarify choices</li></ul>
Brevity	
Top-down Explanation	<ul><li>Practice BLUF</li><li>Use headlines instead of subjects for emails</li><li>Listen to yourself for signs of too much context before getting to the point</li><li>When answering questions, give the short answer first before context</li></ul>

So What Filter	• When planning your arguments, ask so what at least three times • Practice awareness of the Four-I test
Clarity	
Transparent Logic	• Pay attention to your structure • Pause before answering • Mentally outline your answers • Signal your structure up front with verbal or written agendas • Practice using signposts and transitions as you speak • Create templates for your favorite structures
Candor and Directness	• Identify obstacles to candor in your regular conversations • Listen to your and others' levels of candor and directness
User-Friendly Language	• Go through your presentations and identify smoke and FOG • Practice eliminating passive verbs • Read your writing out loud • Think about using language specific to your audience • Illustrate abstract concepts with concrete examples • Check your presentations for stories, analogies and visuals • Pay attention to your own hedges and hesitations • Ask someone to catch your filler words
Dialogue	
Just-in-time Communication	• Monitor your listener's reactions and slow down or speed up as necessary • Practice the 4 + 2 Ps of answering questions • Practice signaling your bullet points up front • Pressure test your ideas before important discussions or presentations • Take words off slides
Lean Questioning	• Prepare questions in advance for critical conversations

Lean Listening	<ul><li>Remind yourself to listen for lean in at least one conversation a day.</li><li>As your counterpart talks, try to extract their bottom line.</li><li>Apply the so what test as you listen.</li><li>Listen for their logical structure.</li><li>Practice the "Plan to Report" hack.</li><li>Listen between the lines for POCR: Problems, Opportunities, Changes and Risks.</li><li>Take stock of your talk-listen ratio</li><li>Consciously use reflecting and responding skills</li><li>Organize your office to reduce distractions</li></ul>
General Improvement	
	<ul><li>Take stock periodically</li><li>Re-read this book</li><li>Recruit a colleague or friend to work with you</li></ul>

Index

Endnotes

Introduction

1 This phrase, as far as I can tell, was coined by Dieter Rams, the famous industrial designer. Except the way he said it was: "*Weniger, aber besser.*"

2 Leonard Reed, "I, Pencil," https://fee.org/resources/i-pencil/

3 Dick Lee and Delmar Hatesohl, "Listening: Our Most-Used Communications Skill," MU Extension, https://extension. missouri.edu/cm150/#:~:text=A%20typical%20study%20 points%20out,speaking%2C%20and%2045%20percent%20 listening.

4 Cited in Thomas H. Davenport and John C. Beck, *The Attention Economy*, p. 11.

5 Craig Fehrman, "The Incredible Shrinking Sound Bite," *Boston Globe*, January 2, 2011. http://archive.boston.com/ bostonglobe/ideas/articles/2011/01/02/the_incredible_shrink- ing_sound_bite/

6 Jerome Groopman, *How Doctors Think*, p. 17.

7 Linda Stone, "Beyond Simple Multi-Tasking: Continuous Partial Attention, https://lindastone.net/2009/11/30/beyond- simple-multi-tasking-continuous-partial-attention/

8   Thomas H. Davenport and John C. Beck, *The Attention Economy.*

9   Bill Jensen, *Simplicity: the New Competitive Advantage in a World of More, Better, Faster*, pp. 24-25.

10 If anyone disagrees, they are at least guilty of #1 in that list.

11 Michael Mankins, "This Weekly Meeting Took Up 300,000 Hours per Year", *Harvard Business Review*, April 29, 2014. https://hbr.org/2014/04/how-a-weekly-meeting-took-up-300000-hours-a-year. Accessed December 14, 2018.

12 "*The Social Economy: Unlocking Productivity through the Use of Social Technologies*", McKinsey Global Institute. http://www.mckinsey.com/insights/high_tech_telecoms_internet/the_social_economy

13 https://www.radicati.com/wp/wp-content/uploads/2015/02/Email-Statistics-Report-2015-2019-Executive-Summary.pdf

14 "*Bad Writing Costs Business Billions*", Josh Bernoff. https://www.thedailybeast.com/bad-writing-costs-businesses-billions Accessed 12/14/18.

15 Daniel Kahneman, Thinking, Fast and Slow, pp. 60-63.

16 "For whosoever hath, to him shall be given, and he shall have more abundance: but whosoever hath not, from him shall be taken away even that he hath." Matthew 13:12

17 See Chapter 4.

Chapter 1

1   Adam Grant, *Give and Take*, p. 89.

2   Carmen Nobel, *Clay Christensen's Milkshake Marketing,* Clay Christensen's Milkshake Marketing - Harvard Business School Working Knowledge (hbs.edu)

3   Seriously. It's called empathy erosion, and it's covered in Chapter 11.

4   Daniel Goleman, Focus: The Hidden Drive of Excellence, p. 113.

5   Gollwitzer, et.al., *Perspective Taking as a Means to Overcome Motivational Barriers in Negotiations: When Putting Oneself Into the Opponent's Shoes Helps to Walk Toward Agreements.* Journal of Personality and Social Psychology, 2011.

6   *Patients' Health Motivates Workers to Wash Their Hands,* Psychological Science, August 29, 2011.

7   Chip Heath and Dan Heath, *Made to Stick*, pp. 187-188.

8   Epley, N., & Caruso, E. M. (2008). Perspective taking: Misstepping into others' shoes. In K. D. Markman, W. M. P. Klein, & J. A. Suhr (Eds.), *The handbook of imagination and mental simulation* (pp. 295-309). New York: Psychology Press.

9   Ulysses S. Grant, *Personal Memoirs of U.S. Grant,* p. 160.

10 A Primer on Decision Making: How Decisions Happen, James March, p.

11 Charles Green, quoted in John Baldoni, "How Trustworthy Are You?," *Harvard Business Review blog*, May 15, 2008.

12 Epley, N., & Caruso, E. M. (2008). Perspective taking: Misstepping into others' shoes. In K. D. Markman, W. M. P. Klein, & J. A. Suhr (Eds.), The handbook of imagination and mental simulation (pp. 295-309).

Chapter 2

1   Daniel Kahneman, *Thinking, Fast and Slow*, pp. 62-67.

2   Sheena Iyengar, *The Art of Choosing*, p. 187.

3   Roy Baumeister and John Tierney, *Willpower*, p. 94.

4   G. Richard Shell and Mario Moussa, *The Art of Woo*, p. 79.

5   Alan H. Palmer, *Talk Lean: Quicker Results, Better Relations*, p. 28.

6   It's called inoculation theory, and it works just like a vaccination. When someone counters your arguments, it strengthens their commitment to their own position.

7   Francis J. Flynn, Vanessa K.B. Lake, "If You Need Help, Just Ask: Underestimating Compliance With Direct Requests for Help", *Journal of Personality and Social Psychology*, 2008.

Brevity

1 You can also be terse but that implies rudeness, which violates the principle of respect for the individual.
2 Josh Bernoff, *Writing Without Bullshit*, p. 5.

Chapter 3

1 Susan M. Weinschenk, *100 Things Every Presenter Needs to Know about People,* p. 100.
2 John Medina, *Brain Rules*, Chapter 4.
3 Legend has it that this practice arose during the Civil War, because the telegraph lines could be cut down at any time, or the army could take precedence over commercial traffic. So reporters learned to get the essentials across as quickly as possible. Even if it's not true, it's a useful metaphor, because the telegraph lines of your listeners' attention can be cut at any time.
4 Bill Lane, *Jacked Up*, p. 293.

Chapter 4

1 Ruth Clark, Frank Nguyen, John Sweller, *Efficiency in Learning*, p. 117.
2 Cited in Marshall Goldsmith, *What Got You Here Won't Get You There*, p. 107.
3 This last admonition is a perfect example. Some may not need the reminder, hence it's irrelevant. Some may need to be constantly reminded, making it integral.
4 Bill Lane, *Jacked Up*, p. 293.
5 John Medina, *Brain Rules*, p. 120.

Clarity

1 Accuracy can be the enemy of clarity, as you can tell by reading almost any legal document.
2 If Einstein has said half the things that are attributed to him, he probably would not have had time to think much about physics.

3 William H. Dubay, *The Principles of Readability*, p. 1.

4 Daniel Kahneman, *Thinking, Fast and Slow*, pp. 62-67.

5 Cutler Dawson, Interview, February 13, 2019. I have not been able to independently corroborate it, but I don't care, because it's such a great story.

6 But don't take this too far. Another great physicist, Richard Feynman, said, "Hell, if I could explain it to the average person, it wouldn't have been worth the Nobel Prize." *Los Angeles Times*, February 16, 1988.

Chapter 5

1 John Shook, "Visual Management – The Good, The Bad, and the Ugly", accessed August 7, 2019.

2 Barbara Minto, *The Pyramid Principle*, p. 12.

3 Leonid Rozenblit and Frank Keil, "The Misunderstood Limits of Folk Science: An Illusion of Explanatory Depth," *Cognitive Science*, September 1, 2002.

4 Barbara Minto, *The Pyramid Principle*, p. 7. Also, note that she was referring to the printed page. It's much more difficult to do these mental operations while listening to a speaker.

5 Dan Markovitz, *If Jon Stewart Can Do It, So Can You* http://www.markovitzconsulting.com/blog/blog/if-jon-stewart-can-do-it-so-can-you?rq=stewart accessed 11/10/15

6 Bruce Gabrielle, *Speaking PowerPoint: The New Language of Business*, p. 10.

Chapter 6

1 Malcolm Gladwell, *Outliers: The Story of Success*, p. 209.

2 Noel Tichy and Ram Charan, "Speed, Simplicity, Self-Confidence: An Interview with Jack Welch," *Harvard Business Review*, September-October 1989.

3 James O'Toole and Warren Bennis, "What's Needed Next: A Culture of Candor," *Harvard Business Review*, June 2009.

4   Another example of being candid but not direct.

5   Deborah Tannen, "The Power of Talk: Who Gets Heard and Why," *Harvard Business Review*, September-October, 1995.

6   The wording in the example is taken from the Wikipedia entry for mitigated speech, and is also to be found in various other blog posts. They reference Gladwell's *Outliers* as well as the following paper, which Gladwell used as a source: Ute Fischer and Judith Orasanu, "Say It Again Sam! Effective Communication Strategies to Mitigate Pilot Error," *Proceedings of the 10th International Symposium on Aviation Psychology*, May 1999. However, I have not been able to find the source of the exact wording at time of publication.

7   It also teaches captains how to recognize the direct message hidden in mitigated speech, which we cover in Lean Listening chapter.

8   It's called primacy and recency effect.

9   Francis J. Flynn and Vanessa K. B. Lake, "If You Need Help, Just Ask: Underestimating Compliance With Direct Requests for Help," *Journal of Personality and Social Psychology*, 2008.

10 You may be familiar with terms such as Amiable, Analytic, Driver and Expressive; or for DISC, the comparable terms are Steadiness, Conscientiousness, Dominance and Influence.

11 Deborah Tannen, "The Power of Talk: Who Gets Heard and Why," *Harvard Business Review*, September-October, 1995.

12 Kim Scott, *Radical Candor: How to Get What You Want by Saying What You Mean.*

13 Tannen, *Power of Talk.*

Chapter 7

1   Plain Language At Work Newsletter, http://www.impact-information.com/impactinfo/newsletter/plwork15.htm

2   DM Oppenheimer, "Consequences of Erudite Vernacular Used Irrespective of Necessity: Problems with Using Long Words Needlessly," *Applied Cognitive Psychology*, 2006.

3 L.J. Rittenhouse, *Investing Between the Lines.* There's a related term, SMOG: Specific Measure of Gobbledygook.

4 Berkshire-Hathaway annual report, 2006.

5 Heath and Heath, *Made to Stick*, p. 116.

6 *Citigroup Eliminates 11,000 Jobs in History's Most Corporate-Jargony Paragraph Ever*, Derek Thompson, The Atlantic, December 5, 2012.

7 Robert Todd Carroll, "Forer Effect", *The Skeptic's Dictionary*, http://skepdic.com/forer.html.

8 Josh Bernoff, *Writing without Bullshit*, p. 76.

9 Dan Pink, *To Sell Is Human*, p. 211.

10 For example: Amanda M. Durik, M. Anne Britt, Rebecca Reynolds, Jennifer Storey, "The Effects of Hedges in Persuasive Arguments," *Journal of Language and Social Psychology*, 2008.

Dialogue

1 William Isaacs, *Dialogue and the Art of Thinking Together*, p. 9.

2 Stanley McChrystal, *Leaders: Myth and Reality*, p. 109.

Chapter 8

1 Steven Pinker, *The Sense of Style*, p. 69.

2 James P. Womack, Daniel T. Jones, *Lean Thinking: Banish Waste and Create Wealth in Your Organization*, p. 71.

3 George A. Miller, "The Magical Number Seven, Plus or Minus Two: Some Limits on Our Capacity for Processing Information," *Psychological Review*, 1956.

4 That's one reason a transparent logical structure is so helpful. See Chapter 5.

5 I'm not advocating "bullet-point thinking", which can be shallow recitation of lists. The difference that I'm talking about here is that a lean communicator *begins* with bullet points, but is prepared to go as deep as necessary to elaborate and defend them.

Chapter 9

1 For example, see: Neil Rackham, *SPIN Selling*; Andrew Finlayson, *Questions that Work*; L. David Marquet, *Leadership Is Language*; and Schein, cited below.

2 See either one of these works by Edgar H. Schein: *Humble Inquiry: The Gentle Art of Asking Instead of Telling*, or *Helping: How to Offer, Give and Receive Help*.

3 Jeffrey Pfeffer, "The Smart Talk Trap", *Harvard Business Review*, May-June 1999.

4 Gollwitzer, P. M., Wieber, F., Myers, A. L., & McCrea, S. M. (2010). *How to maximize implementation intention effects.* In book: *Then a miracle occurs: Focusing on behavior in social psychological theory and research* (p. 137–161).

5 For example, Peter R. Scholtes, *The Leader's Handbook*.

6 Mary Budd Rowe, "Wait Time: Slowing Down May Be A Way of Speeding Up!," *Journal of Teacher Education*, 1986.

Chapter 10

1 Lee and Hatesohl, ibid.

2 Peggy Johnson, Interview, August 14, 2019.

3 The key phrase is "you're the driver".

4 For a visual demonstration of selective attention, check out http://www.theinvisiblegorilla.com/gorilla_experiment.html

5 These specific terms come from Barker and Watson's listening styles model. See James B. Weaver, Kittie W. Watson, Larry L. Barker, "Individual Differences in Listening Styles: Do You Hear What I Hear?," *Personality and Individual Differences*, March 1996.

Chapter 11

1 Deborah Barrett, "Leadership Communication: A Communication Approach for Senior-Level Managers," https://www.academia.edu/8605392/Leadership_Communication_-_

Leadership_Communication_A_Communication_Approach_ for_Senior-Level_Managers_Barrett

2   Steve Dakolios, Interview, February 27, 2019.

3   Jeffrey Pfeffer, "Why We Absolve Successful People—and Companies—of Bad Behavior," *Insights by Stanford Business*, June 16, 2016.

4   Dacher Keltner, *The Power Paradox: How We Gain and Lose Influence*, p. 101.

5   Galinsky et. al., "Power and Perspectives Not Taken," *Psychological Science*, 2006.

6   Heidi Grant Halvorson, *No One Understands You, and What to Do About It*, p. 92.

7   Travis Bradberry, "Results or People: Where Should a Leader Focus?," *Forbes* 12/23/16.

8   Jim Harter and Annamarie Mann, "The Right Culture: Not Just About Employee Satisfaction," *Workplace*, April 12, 2017.

9   Daniel Goleman, Richard Boyatzis, Annie McKee, *Primal Leadership: Learning to Lead with Emotional Intelligence*, p. 8.

10   Cited in Robert H. Gass and John S. Seiter, *Persuasion, Social Influence and Compliance Gaining*, p. 200.

11   Jeffrey Pfeffer, *What Were They Thinking?: Unconventional Wisdom about Management*, p. 104.

12   Brandon Rigoni and Bailey Nelson, "Do Employees Really Know What's Expected of Them?," *Business Journal*, September 27, 2016.

13   Brian Westfall, "Why Honesty Is the Secret Ingredient of Successful Organizations," *Software Advice blog*, April 24, 2017.

14   David Epstein shares valuable lessons from these episodes in his book *Range: Why Generalists Triumph in A Specialized World*, Chapter 11.

15   David Epstein, *Range: Why Generalists Triumph in A Specialized World*, p. 262.

Chapter 12

1 James Clear, *Atomic Habits*; and Eben Harrell, "How 1% Improvements Led to Olympic Gold," *Harvard Busines Review*, October 30, 2015.
2 Peter Gollwitzer, "Implementation Intentions: Strong Effects of Simple Plans," *American Psychologist*, July, 1999.

The Books of Wisdom/Work

Wisdom/Work is a new cooperative, cutting edge imprint and resource for publishing books by practical philosophers and innovative thinkers who can have a positive cultural impact in our time. We turn the procedures of traditional publishing upside down and put more power, a vastly higher speed of delivery, and greater rewards into the hands of our authors.

The imprint was launched with the Morris Institute for Human Values, founded by Tom Morris (Ph.D. Yale), a former professor of philosophy at Notre Dame and a public philosopher who has given over a thousand talks on the wisdom of the ages. Wisdom/Work was established to serve both his audiences and the broader culture. From the imprint's first projects, it began to attract the attention of other authors who seek to expand their positive influence.

Wisdom/Work occupies a distinctive territory outside most traditional publishing domains. Its main concern is high quality expedited production and release, with affordability for buyers. We seek to serve a broad audience of intelligent readers with the best of ancient and modern wisdom. Subjects will touch on such issues as success, ethics, happiness, meaning, work, and how best to live a good life.

As an imprint, we have created a process for working with a few high quality projects a year compatible with our position in the market, and making available to our authors a well-guided and streamlined process for launching their books into the world. For more information, email Tom Morris, Editor-in-Chief, through his reliable address of: TomVMorris@aol.com. You can also learn more at the editor's website, www.TomVMorris.com.

www.ingramcontent.com/pod-product-compliance
Lightning Source LLC
Chambersburg PA
CBHW031406180326
41458CB00043B/6637/J